TRUST THE PEOPLE

TRUST THE PEOPLE

The Selected Essays and Speeches of PETER WALKER

Edited by Neale Stevenson

With an introduction by Robert Rhodes James

COLLINS
8 Grafton Street, London W1
1987

William Collins Sons & Co. Ltd
London · Glasgow · Sydney · Auckland
Toronto · Johannesburg

ISBN 0-00-217637-8

First published 1987

Photoset in Linotron Times by
Rowland Phototypesetting Ltd
Bury St Edmunds, Suffolk
Made and printed in Great Britain by
Robert Hartnoll (1985) Ltd, Bodmin, Cornwall

To Tessa, Jonathan, Shara
Timothy, Robin and Marianne
to whom he owes so much

Contents

'Trust the people' – I have long tried to make that my motto . . . the Tory party of today is no longer identified with that small and narrow class which is connected with the ownership of land; but that its great strength can be found, and must be developed, in our large towns as well as in our country districts. Yes, trust the people. You, who are ambitious, and rightly ambitious, of being the guardians of the British Constitution, trust the people, and they will trust you – and they will follow you and join you in the defence of that Constitution against any and every foe. I have no fear of democracy.

LORD RANDOLPH CHURCHILL,
Birmingham, 16 April 1884

INTRODUCTION

by ROBERT RHODES JAMES, M.P.

To an extent that is often insufficiently realized, everyone in public life or with a keen interest in public affairs is the recipient, for good or ill, of his or her formative experiences and influences. For my father's generation, which was that of Anthony Eden and Harold Macmillan, it was the searing ordeal of the Great War; they survived, but too many of their friends did not. But they had also seen how people from totally different backgrounds could fight and work together in a common cause, and asked themselves why this could not be achieved in peace. One Nation Conservatism has deep roots, but in our century it has been the actual experience on two occasions of what a united nation can do that is its modern inspiration.

Both Peter Walker and I are children of the 1930s, born under the shadow of war and brought up in its actuality. He then did National Service, and was shocked by the clear difference between officers and men, a divide based not on ability or courage but on social background. He found that his fellow-soldiers were highly intelligent but woefully ill-educated. This personal experience drew him towards the kind of Conservatism for which Harold Macmillan and Iain Macleod stood, although at the beginning of his political career he was a prominent opponent of our entry into the Common Market – in my view wrongly, and perhaps the influence of Leo Amery and the shadow of Joseph Chamberlain had much to do with that youthful error! It was very natural that he should have been so attracted to John and Robert Kennedy, whose refreshing 'can do' philosophy exhilarated millions of non-Americans, and which has never fully revived, although, as he shrewdly points out, it could be that Gorbachev could do it for the Soviet Union and awaken that slumbering and unhappy giant.

Peter Walker's fundamental political philosophy has never wavered, although inevitably it has been tempered by further experiences as a senior Minister. His basic optimism also contains realism, as in his wise warnings against the claim that the revival of industrial and business prosperity can be achieved by small businesses alone, and in his determined and sensitive handling of the miners' strike. A notable feature of this grim but crucial episode was the care and skill with which he kept all his colleagues informed of developments and put the case to the nation and to the miners themselves with such ability and seriousness that, albeit at heavy cost, the threat to our society and our institutions – and which was a very real one – was decisively defeated. It was as good an example of any of that 'grace under fire' that John F. Kennedy so much admired. The manner in which Peter Walker dealt with the well-meaning but confused and naïve maunderings of the Bishop of Durham also deserves to be noted.

In this selection from his writings and speeches certain themes recur, and quite rightly, especially that of unemployment. His attitude and remedies require careful and sympathetic attention, but particularly his insistence that it is unacceptable. He will not have it that this situation must be with us permanently and accepted resignedly. That is not the approach of the One Nation Conservative, and never has been. It is this vital strand that takes us back to Lord Randolph Churchill's Tory Democracy, the warnings and social programmes of Disraeli, the dedication of Shaftesbury, and the vision of Peel. New problems and new challenges confront us, but the politician with a heart is always the one to watch, to study, and to profit from.

It is a personal honour and pleasure for me to commend this book most warmly to all who care for our people and their future and who wish to be involved in the new British Revolution, which can only be achieved by that liberal and progressive Conservatism for which Peter Walker has always stood.

EDITOR'S INTRODUCTION

At Oxford I found that Peter Walker exercised an unrivalled influence over the younger activists of the Conservative Party. This was surprising, for his views and political approach were noticeably out of line with the new monetarist dogmas that were then fashionable within the Conservative Party.

Peter Walker is the leading politician in the Conservative Party who has consistently steered the middle path between the facile assumptions of socialist planning and the mystic calvinism of the free marketeers.

In economics as in politics he believes that government fails unless it makes capitalism work for the people. He wishes to give to all sections of society a stake in the capitalist economy. He is the leading voice to achieve universal property ownership, wider share ownership, and an increased share in the profits and responsibilities of the people in their workplace. He recognizes the high priority to the family of a good health service, a good house and the best in education.

It has been a remarkable political life. He was Chairman of a Young Conservatives branch at fourteen. When he became National Chairman of the Young Conservatives he was then the youngest person to have reached that position. He fought his first parliamentary election at the age of twenty-two. He was adopted for a Conservative seat at the age of twenty-eight. He was the youngest member of the front bench within three years of entering parliament. He was the youngest member of the Shadow Cabinet, and the youngest member of the Cabinet, and now, as his speeches and writings show, is still positive about the future.

I have been keen for some time to gather in a published

form the various political subjects that Peter Walker has addressed. This book brings together lessons from the past, including the unique experience Peter Walker has had as the Minister at the centre of the coal dispute of 1984/5.

Peter Walker speaks here of his hopes of a future with a less alienated and more participatory society – where all have access to work, all can take shares in their firms and own their own homes, where all have the absolute conviction that they stand to gain by the growth of the national economy.

Further, he feels that economic and social trends mean that we can only sustain economic growth and maintain social stability by matching material gains by an increase in the *quality* of the lives that we all lead. His concern is that we should recognize that these are non-material contributions we can and should make and that the real definition of a fulfilling life depends as much on expanding opportunities for education and leisure in the 'civilized, opportunity society'.

His view of the future is a society with the correct balance between compassion and efficiency. He seeks to create a nation where community and family values are cherished, and where every individual has the opportunity to participate in all aspects of national life.

1

Influences

Peter Walker recently celebrated twenty-five years as Member of Parliament for Worcester. Reflecting on his quarter of a century in Parliament, his delight at being involved in the political process was undisguised. He still savours the moment when the Returning Officer announced that Peter Walker had been elected, and he does not hide the fact that that night in Worcester represented the achievement of his greatest ambition in life since the age of thirteen.

Walker's political beliefs were shaped during the War and in the immediate post-war years by what he describes as 'a primitive but enthusiastic patriotism'. Aged seven when war broke out, his was a patriotism fed by Churchill's war-time broadcasts, and fostered by the sense of national purpose which he experienced in the air-raid shelters of suburban London.

Political controversy came later, but Walker's first memories are of a society totally united in the pursuit of an agreed goal. This sense of the strength of a united nation, which he first experienced as a schoolboy, is a thread which recurs in Walker's speeches and writings. His book, The Ascent of Britain, *opens with a chapter entitled 'The Role of Patriotism' in which he writes:*

Some would argue that the passing of national greatness is to be welcomed. Those cosmopolitan 'friends of every country but their own' so bitterly assailed by Disraeli are happy to reinforce a mood of self-doubt and lack of confidence. They are, however, involved in a dangerous enterprise. Political thinkers of both left and right have long recognized the force of patriotism. Writing in 1940, George

Orwell saw patriotism as a network of feelings and loyalties which served to preserve our identity, our sense of what we were. 'In England,' Orwell wrote, 'patriotism takes different forms in different classes, but it runs like a connecting thread through nearly all of them. Only the Europeanized intelligentsia are really immune to it.'

For a nation patriotism represents a unique cohesive factor, binding a nation together and giving it strength. Patriotism represents the highest unifying factor that a nation can possess on a secular level.

My own political thinking was very much affected by reading Lord Milner's definition of patriotism. According to him, patriotism meant that at home you pursued policies the object of which was to see that every person born to be a citizen of your country rejoiced in that birthright. This, he argued, meant pursuing policies of social reform that would eventually eradicate poverty and squalor.

The restoration of a national patriotism is of vital importance in its effect upon the individual. When patriotism departs, cynicism enters. The individual seems to have less desire to be creative – and it is the aggregate desire of individual citizens to be creative that brings about the advancement of a nation's resources.

Walker was introduced to Lord Milner's ideas by a Conservative politician who had worked closely with Milner in his own youth – Leo Amery. As Walker later wrote, 'It was a stroke of good fortune for me that I met Leo Amery, one of our most distinguished pre-war statesmen when in my early teens. I had just made a speech at the Conservative Party Conference, and he was kind enough to encourage me in my political activities. From time to time he invited me to his home in Eaton Square. He talked to me of his experiences and I enjoyed the benefit of his very considerable political wisdom. He gave me books to read and spoke to me about the figures from the past that had made an impression on him.'

Those conversations with Leo Amery undoubtedly made a deep impression on the young Peter Walker. By the time they met Amery was an elder statesman of the Conservative Party and the most senior exponent of the imperial idea. As a young man he had been active in the circle which included Lord Milner, and which acknowledged Joseph Chamberlain as its leader. Throughout his career Amery kept alive Chamberlain's commitment to a reforming domestic policy and an assertive foreign policy. Walker's link through Amery to Chamberlain is clear in the passage in The Ascent of Britain *in which Walker describes, with obvious approval, Chamberlain's approach to politics.*

Chamberlain's background as an outsider in politics, a businessman amongst landowners and lawyers, a provincial amongst Londoners, meant that he was able to see the implications of political doctrines at the grass roots rather than relying upon inherited knowledge, or the textbooks of political economy. What was required, he argued in the debate over the tariff, was 'not the deductive reasoning of the professors, but the inductive reasoning of hard facts'. Chamberlain moved with the times; he abandoned doctrines when they became irrelevant to the facts of industrial experience. His central contribution to Conservative thought was his instinctive realization at the beginning of the twentieth century that Britain's industrial dominance was gone for good; that the 'informal empire' based upon Britain's control of the seas and financial leadership was no longer sufficient to make her a dominant power; that in twentieth-century geo-politics those states with access to large markets would inevitably exert the greatest influence.

In January 1885, while still a Liberal, Chamberlain said, 'how to promote the greatest happiness of the masses of the people, how to increase their enjoyment of life, that is the problem of the future'. He was the first statesman to concentrate his whole energies upon social and economic reform, the first leading politician to favour the creative use of political power to improve the standard of living of the masses.

But Chamberlain realized that it would be impossible to

secure any lasting improvement in the standard of living of the British working classes without guaranteeing Britain's trade position. That is why he came to support tariff reform, a scheme to ensure Britain's access to imperial markets. Similarly, in our own day Conservatives have supported the idea of a wider European patriotism to replace the nineteenth-century imperial dream.

With an assured market for Britain's industry, production and employment could be maintained. Chamberlain proposed to finance old age pensions out of the proceeds of protective duties. But the keystone of his policies was the security that tariff reform offered as an alternative to the constant dislocations and instabilities of the world economy.

There was then a direct link between the programme of social reform and the programme of strengthening Britain's position abroad; as Chamberlain's supporter, Lord Milner, argued, 'amongst civilisations placed of more or less equal size, that one will be, as it will deserve to be, the strongest, which is most successful in removing the causes of class antagonism in its midst'. Chamberlain, like Disraeli, sought to oppose Marxist materialism through imaginative and constructive new policies. If these changes were not carried out, Chamberlain foresaw the growth of a socialist movement. Such a movement did not frighten him, however, for he saw it as basically defensive, a movement to secure working class rights in the face of trade depression, but without a constructive policy for dealing with the economic difficulties.

The mainstream of British Conservatism has rarely been reactionary, resisting all change, as some continental parties of the right have been. The historian A. J. P. Taylor has said unkindly, 'what has called itself Conservatism in the last hundred years has merely consented not to be a brake on the march of progress. Past Conservatism has defended the Liberal achievements of the previous generation.'

Joseph Chamberlain certainly did not hold this conception of Conservatism. He wanted to transform the Conservative Party from a party of sound administration and cautious, ameliorative reform into one with a positive and dynamic creed. This creed would avoid the dangers of class conflict inherent in the Conservatism of the market economy. Chamberlain's policy was one of class harmony, both worker and capitalist alike were held to have a stake in Britain's prosperity. For the capitalist, tariff reform offered secure markets and a balanced climate for expansion. For the worker, it offered high wages and, above all, the security of full employment. Thus Chamberlain attempted to alter the accepted categories of British politics by securing a drastic political realignment of the classes and a new electoral coalition for the Conservative Party.

Apart from introducing Walker to the ideas of Joseph Chamberlain, Leo Amery also encouraged him to read widely among Conservative philosophers, particularly Edmund Burke, whose writings stress the importance of a practical approach to Government. Once again, Walker's philosophical debt is clear in the passage in The Ascent of Britain *in which he discusses Burke.*

Burke's central theme was an attack upon the arrogance of what he called 'private reason', the arrogance of the intellectual who believes that he can reform society without taking notice of the collective feelings of his compatriots, or the history of the society in which he lives; what he was attacking was very much like the ideology of the Marxist, socialist, or believer in extreme *laissez-faire* of our own day. For, just as in the eighteenth century, men believed that the scientific discoveries of the Enlightenment enabled them to plan the future development of society, so, in our own time, the development of Marxism has led many to believe that politics can be reduced to ideology.

Burke's ideology was that every man's private reasonings must be carefully checked against the evidence of the similar reasonings of others in his society, and against the particular traditions of that society. For institutions which might well work in one society would not necessarily work if transplanted into another. Burke applied this analysis in his defence of the American colonists against George III, when he argued that it was vital to govern America according to the circumstances created by history and geography, and 'not according to abstract ideas of right, by no means according to mere general themes of government, the resort to which appears to me, in our present situation, no better than arrant trifling'.

Later Burke attacked the French Revolution precisely because the French had not adopted the empirical methods of the American colonists and had ignored the need for practical reforms through their excessive attachment to ideology. Burke compared the French Revolution with the 'Glorious Revolution' of 1688 in Britain. Why was it that the French Revolution led to bloodshed and tyranny while the English revolution led to a more practical defence of existing liberties? Burke saw that this was because the English preserved what they were not compelled to destroy; although they departed from the precedents of history they did so with great reluctance. Burke was not hostile to reform, he was by no means an unthinking reactionary, but he realized that when something new was created legitimacy for it could only be obtained by absorbing it into a national tradition which had already existed for some time. That is the principle that was neglected in the French and Russian revolutions. Those revolutions lacked men with the ability to improve and the disposition to preserve, which Burke saw as the hallmark of a great statesman. Burke did not believe there were any general laws of politics, and, as he argued in *Reflections on the Revolution in France*, 'circumstances (which for some gentlemen pass for nothing) give in reality to every political principle its distinguishing colour and discriminating effect. The circumstances are what render every civil and political scheme beneficial or noxious to mankind.' Thus it is that there is no contradiction in the Conservative supporting the American revolution but opposing the French; or in supporting state intervention in the nineteenth century while being, on the whole, opposed to it today in the twentieth century. It is, as Burke realized, all a matter of 'circumstances'.

Burke noticed the central principle of Conservatism, namely that every political system and every constitution is a balance between opposing elements, a balance between reform and preservation. Either extreme is likely to be mistaken: too rapid and too radical reform is dangerous, just as there is a danger in retaining the *status quo* after it has ceased to have any real justification. Radicals commonly underestimate the first of these dangers, and continental right-wingers the second. In his *Reflections on the Revolution in France* Burke argued that 'a state without the means of some change, is without the means of its conservation'. It is the reforming nature of British Conservatism that has saved it from the fate of many continental right-wing parties doomed to remain permanent minorities in their own countries.

Government for Burke involved essentially the practical problem of how to rule equitably in the historical circumstances facing a country. Government, he argued, is 'a practical thing made for the happiness of mankind, and not to furnish it a spectacle of uniformity, to gratify the schemes of visionary politicians'.

It is, then, in his understanding of the practical nature of politics that Burke's importance to present-day Conservatives lies. His theory of balance, his awareness of the connections between tradition and reform, and his distrust of ideology all make him a founding father of Conservative thinking.

Peter Walker's brand of practical patriotism continued to develop as he reached manhood. Like all his contemporaries, he had to do two years' National Service, and like many at the time, he found his period in the Army deepened his understanding of his fellow countrymen. His experience of National Service emphasized to him the divisions which still existed in British society, and which he felt violated the concept of the nation which was fostered both by Churchill during the war and by his later contacts with Amery. In the evolution of his political ideas his experiences during his time in National Service undoubtedly played a significant part. As he later wrote of his time as a National Serviceman.

The ghastly waste of human resources that results from our educational and industrial system is perhaps one of the worst features of British life. I was first made aware of this by my experiences as a National Serviceman. As an eighteen-year-old I had no concept of military life. A number of my uncles had served as soldiers during the war, but my father had been too old, and I had no relatives who had ever pursued a military career until my brother joined the navy as an artificer at the age of fifteen. I did not gather from him the difference between being commissioned and non-commissioned, nor did I understand the way in which the army was rigidly divided into officers and men. I did not know that the officers came from one social background and the men from another, and that only a small fraction of the men who joined the ranks ever became officers. There was the rare case of the warrant officer who was commissioned, but the division between officers and men was not based upon ability. It was a division in which there was unfair opportunity.

When I did my two years' National Service I had no idea that with my educational background I would have been wise to have applied to become a commissioned officer. When I was interviewed for my National Service I was asked what regiment I wished to go into. I was in considerable difficulty as I didn't know the names of any regiments and knew little of the diverse sections of the army. I had heard that there was an Educational Corps, however, and I mentioned this and so became an educational instructor in the army.

At the age of eighteen I was suddenly surrounded by young people of similar ability and intellect but with a totally dissimilar social and educational background. I did my basic training with the King's Royal Rifle Corps at Winchester, where for some administrative reason they had suddenly called up a number of young porters from Covent Garden, who all went into one platoon of their own. One of them was called Walker, and when his name got mixed with mine I spent six weeks in the company of the Covent Garden porters.

I soon appreciated their immense wit, keen intelligence and total lack of education. I wrote letters home for some, and filled in forms for others. There was a low standard of literacy but a high standard of intelligence. When later I was posted to the Cheshire Regiment and then to a small unit of the Armoured Corps in Westmorland and I was responsible for the education of the men in these establishments, I discovered quickly that these were men who could be inspired to study for the first time in their lives.

A number of them have had far fuller lives purely because at the age of nineteen or twenty they were encouraged to apply their talents to acquire a better standard of literacy and thereafter to obtain some appropriate qualification that would put them on a new route through life. I realized then that if the small fraction of people that I came across during those two years were typical of the nation as a whole, we were a nation in which much ability was wasted, not developed or never applied, a nation in which the social background of the individual was of far more importance to his future prospects than his ability and intelligence.

By the time he left the Army, therefore, Peter Walker's political personality was beginning to emerge. He had experienced both the privations and the sense of purpose of wartime London as the schoolboy son of a factory worker. After the war he had been tutored in the distinctive approach to politics of Joseph Chamberlain by his greatest living disciple, Leo Amery. But his time as a National Serviceman had demonstrated to the young Walker that the social objectives embraced by Chamberlain were still well short of achievement. Despite a century's progress the stranger might still talk of 'two nations; between whom there is no intercourse and no sympathy; who are as ignorant of each other's habits, thoughts and feelings as if they were dwellers in different zones, or inhabitants of different planets; who are formed by a different breeding, are fed by a different food, are ordered by different manners, and are not governed by the same laws' (Disraeli).

Peter Walker does not simply find social division and discrimination offensive in themselves; he believes they sap the strength of the nation and undermine its moral legitimacy. To condone their existence is therefore unpatriotic.

Walker found that these attitudes were shared by the Conservative leadership of the time. After the collapse of the wartime coalition Churchill had insisted that the party continue to occupy the centre ground of British politics. Lord Woolton's slogan had been 'we not only cope, but we care'. Rab Butler, at Conservative Research Department, produced an avalanche of thorough policy documents which captured for the Party the popular trust it needed. With initiatives such as the Workers Charter and the Industrial Charter, the Conservative Party set down its commitment to a positive and patriotic industrial policy and focused on ensuring for the worker a more fulfilling and dignified participation in employment.

During the 1950s Peter Walker stood twice for Parliament as Conservative candidate in Dartford and rose to be National Chairman of the Young Conservatives. At the end of 1960, at the age of twenty-eight, he was selected as candidate at the impending by-election in Worcester.

The emergence of Peter Walker as Member of Parliament for Worcester was a happy coincidence. His most important link with the city, since his parents moved to Gloucester in 1948, was his keen support for the Worcestershire County Cricket Club. But the closeness of Worcester to Birmingham, the Parliamentary home of both Leo Amery and the Chamberlain family, and the links between Worcester and Elgar, whose music gives English patriotism one of its finest expressions, make the link between Peter Walker and the city of Worcester a happy one at many different levels.

Peter Walker made his home in Worcestershire and has grown deeply attached to the county and its people. He feels that the community that exists in the county comes close to his patriotic ideal. He feels that there is genuine social mobility, and that society is based on real and recognized obligations as well as rights. He regards it as a model which should be repeated elsewhere in Britain.

Walker sees no conflict between his belief in the importance of patriotism and his belief in the importance of Britain's alliance with the United States. Far from it. The 1950s were a time when the 'special relationship' between Britain and the United States was felt to be a very real force. Walker's political apprenticeship with Leo Amery had stressed the importance of an international outlook to politics which meant that he quickly became fully aware of the importance to European security both of the Marshall plan and American economic assistance, and European reliance on the military strength of the United States to resist Soviet expansionism.

As a convinced supporter of the Anglo-American Alliance, and as a business man who during the 1950s built extensive contacts in the American business community, it was therefore natural that Walker should develop an absorbing interest in the domestic politics of the United States. He believes that it is important for European politicians not only to understand the importance to themselves of the American Alliance, but also to understand the domestic political pressures to which American politicians are subject. His fascination with American politics took him to both the Democratic and Republican Conventions in 1952, and to every succeeding Convention of both parties until 1968. It was inevitable that this exposure to American political methods and thinking should influence Walker's own approach to politics.

By far the most important American influence on Walker was however his contact with the Kennedy brothers. He first met John Kennedy when he was a Massachusetts Senator and was deeply impressed both by his attractive style and personality, and by his strong commitment to social reform. He felt that the Kennedy brothers had something important to say to America at the end of the 1950s, and he found their political approach enormously attractive. His support for John

Kennedy led him to join the Primary election campaign team when John Kennedy sought the Democratic nomination for President in 1960.

Walker's debt to the Kennedy brothers was made very clear when on 22nd November, 1983, twenty years after the President's assassination, he delivered the Kennedy Memorial Lecture at the Oxford Union. The lecture reflects on the positive approach of the Kennedy brothers and the ambitious objectives they set for themselves. It contrasts the Kennedy approach with the minimalist lack of ambition espoused by many politicians in the 1980s.

KENNEDY MEMORIAL LECTURE

Oxford Union on Tuesday, 22nd November, 1983

When Jack Kennedy was elected President of the United States I was twenty-eight. Like many others of my generation I had worked on his election campaign and his victory unleashed for me as for millions of others around the world a tide of euphoria which set the new frontier apart from any other political campaign in which I have participated. After the drab fatalism of the Eisenhower years the Free World seemed to have found a leader who was at once both a realist and an optimist, who understood the complexity of the problems he faced, but regarded those problems not as an excuse for inaction, but as a challenge to human intellect and human inventiveness.

For many of us who shared the excitement of Kennedy's victory, his death ushered in an era of drift and hopelessness which has intensified as the years have passed. As Kennedy's Presidency passed into history his infectious optimism seemed everywhere in retreat. His successors seem to tell us only of the problems – never of the solutions. So are we now to conclude that his optimism was misplaced? How can we?

Are we condemned to accept the arms race? Must we learn to tolerate the divide between the developed and developing countries of the world? Must we watch helpless as our economic system absorbs our resources and destroys our environment? Is there nothing we can do to reduce the tension in our inner cities? Are these man-made problems beyond the power of man to solve? Or does the record and example of Jack Kennedy and his brother Bobby have something vital to say to us today? Can their brand of positive disciplined and imaginative leadership offer us solutions to the problems of the 1980s, as it so clearly seemed to do twenty years ago?

Jack and Bobby Kennedy should always be considered together. They were a partnership. Both sought to turn dreams into reality. Both combined righteous anger with quick humour. Both aspired to public service as the highest form of human activity. Both had the ambition to succeed, and the courage to win.

Both were influenced by a father who set high standards and a mother devoted to her family displaying an affection strengthened by a depth of religious belief, a passion for education and a demand for discipline. All the Kennedy campaigns were family campaigns.

The Appeal to Youth

As a campaigner Jack was cool and convincing. His eloquence and gallantry, combined with his humour, was tailor-made for the young at heart. I can personally vouch for the impact on young people of the Kennedy appeal.

Bobby Kennedy spelled out that appeal when he suggested: 'Our answer is the world's hope; it is to rely on youth – not a time of life but a state of mind, a temper of the will, a quality of the imagination, a pre-dominance of courage over timidity, of the appetite for adventure over the love of ease. The cruelties and obstacles of this swiftly changing planet will not yield to obsolete dogmas and outworn slogans. It cannot be moved by those who cling to a present that is already dying, who prefer the illusion of security to the excitement and danger that come with even the most peaceful progress. It is a revolutionary world we live in; and this generation, at home and around the world, has had thrust upon it a greater burden of responsibility than any nation that has ever lived.'

This was a time of protest marches, demonstrations, and riots. The Kennedys, more than any post-war leaders, endeavoured to turn this anger and dissent into constructive reform. Consider Bobby Kennedy's message to the undergraduates of the Sixties: 'It is not enough to allow dissent. We must demand it. For there is much to dissent from . . . Yet we must, as thinking men, distinguish between the right of dissent and the way we choose to exercise that right . . . that dissent which consists simply of sporadic and dramatic acts sustained by neither continuing labour or research – that dissent which seeks to demolish while lacking both the desire and direction for rebuilding, that dissent which, contemptuously or out of laziness, casts aside the practical weapons and instruments of change and progress – that kind of dissent is merely self-indulgence. It is satisfying, perhaps, to those who make it. But it will not solve the problems of our society. It will not assist those seriously engaged in the difficult and frustrating work of the nation. And, when it is all over, it will not have brightened or enriched the life of a single portion of humanity in a single part of the globe.'

Peace the Objective

Jack Kennedy was never in any doubt that the West needed military strength to deter any Soviet temptation to impose Communism by force.

He stopped the missiles in Cuba. He increased defence spending. But he also worked, as no other American leader has worked, to achieve a peaceful relationship with the Soviet Union. The Test Ban Treaty. Dialogue with Soviet leaders. The encouragement to uncommitted nations to believe in the West. These were his achievements and they were signalled in a clear message at the start of his Presidency. 'So let us begin anew – remembering on both sides that civility is not a sign of weakness, and sincerity is always subject to proof. Let us never negotiate out of fear. But let us never fear to negotiate.

'Let both sides seek to invoke the wonders of science

instead of its terrors. Together let us explore the stars, conquer the deserts, eradicate disease, tap the ocean depths and encourage the arts and commerce.'

To the Soviet Union he said: 'To those nations who would make themselves our adversary, we offer not a pledge but a request: That both sides begin anew the quest for peace, before the dark powers of destruction unleashed by science engulf all humanity in planned or accidental self-destruction.

'We dare not tempt them with weakness. For only when our arms are sufficient beyond doubt can we be certain beyond doubt that they will never be employed.

'But neither can two great and powerful groups of nations take comfort from our present course – both sides are over-burdened by the cost of modern weapons, both rightly alarmed by the steady spread of the deadly atom, yet both racing to alter that uncertain balance of terror that stays the hand of mankind's final war.'

Jack Kennedy saw multilateral disarmament not as a debating point but as a political priority. While maintaining a readiness for war, he followed every avenue for peace. He believed that the making of peace was the noblest work of God-fearing men. As Pierre Salinger wrote: 'He brought to a cynical world the hope that a better life was possible. Perhaps it was his youth, his eloquence or his undeniable commitment to life and excellence. But whatever it was, it let a new hope into the hearts of people everywhere that the forces of reason, not the forces of arms, might finally prevail in the councils of men.'

The North–South Challenge

If President Kennedy recognized the importance of security he also understood that the concept of security is meaningless if it is defined in purely military terms.

In 1959, nearly twenty-five years ago, after mentioning the national preoccupation with the missile gap, Kennedy called attention to another gap which he said 'Constitutes an equally clear and present danger to our society – the gap in living standards, income and hope for the future between the stable, industrialized nations of the North and the over-populated, undeveloped nations of the South'. He went on: 'It is this gap which presents us with our most critical challenge today. It is this gap which is altering the face of the globe, our strategy, our security and our alliances more than any current military challenge. And it is this economic challenge to which we have responded most sporadically, most timidly and most inadequately.'

Perhaps there is no more graphic illustration of the failure of governments over the last twenty-five years to address the fundamental issues of our generation than our record in dealing with the Third World. Kennedy's description of the position in 1959 rings as true today as it did when it was first delivered.

Neither the United States nor the European Community have been able to develop the agriculture of the Third World or find ways of channelling the food surpluses of the West to those who are starving.

More than half the human race still lives in conditions of degrading squalor and poverty, while the rich countries of the world appear confident to pass by on the other side. Not only are we apparently careless of the chasm which divides our living standards from those less fortunate than ourselves: We are content in the process to corner for ourselves a disproportionate and ever increasing share of the world's diminishing resources. The Kennedy brothers both understood that that position cannot endure. Twenty years ago Bobby said: 'These people will not accept this kind of existence for the next generation. We would not: They will not. There will be changes. So a revolution is coming – a revolution which will be peaceful if we are wise enough: Compassionate if we care enough: Successful if we are fortunate enough – but a revolution which is coming whether we will it or not. We can affect its character: We cannot alter its inevitability.'

It was that understanding which also led his brother to say at his inauguration: 'To those people in the huts and villages of half the globe struggling to break the bonds of mass misery, we pledge our best efforts to help them help themselves, for whatever period is required – not because the Communists may be doing it, not because we seek their votes, but because it is right. If a free society cannot help the many who are poor, it cannot save the few who are rich.'

I believe it is high time that pledge was renewed.

As in the quest for peace, so in the mission to eradicate poverty, we have failed to fulfil the Kennedy dreams.

Towards a Better Quality of Life

At home the Kennedys realized the need for growth but they recognized the achievement was not a production figure or a monetary target. The objective of growth was an achievement of a better quality of life.

They argued that the gross national product included air pollution, cigarette advertising and ambulances. It included locks for our doors, and jails for the people who break them. It included the destruction of the redwoods and the death of life in Lake Superior. Production figures were boosted by the production of missiles and nuclear warheads. The gross national product swelled with the equipment for the police to put down riots.

They argued too that the gross national product did not include any calculation for the health of the family, the quality of education, the joy of children's play. It was indifferent to the indecency in our factories and the safety on the streets. It had no calculation for the beauty of poetry, the strength of marriages and the integrity of public officials. There was no measure for the justness in dealings with each other. The gross national product measured neither wit nor courage, wisdom nor learning, compassion nor devotion to country. In short it measured everything except everything which makes life worthwhile.

Just as the Kennedy brothers' central message in foreign affairs was that mankind could be the master of its circumstances and not the victim, so in domestic politics they believed that the solution to the problems of poverty, disease and racial disadvantage lay in the creative ability of a free people.

The Inner Cities

Both brothers found it offensive that there still existed within the world's wealthiest society ghettos of chronic social and economic deprivation. They believed that the development of the economies of America's inner cities, like the development of Third World economies, demanded attention because the *status quo* was both a threat to national interests and an affront to national morality.

Yet they also recognized that social improvements could only be obtained through economic growth – that governments had a special duty to minorities who did not possess the political clout to enable them to exert much influence on the system. They rejected the sterility of Socialism, they foreswore bureaucratic social engineering, they recognized that social improvements could only be obtained by economic growth and they therefore sought to fertilize and then to harness the creative energies of a free economy. Theirs was an entirely practical approach; just as Harold Macmillan learnt in Stockton-on-Tees to seek what he called 'The Middle Way' so the Kennedy brothers learnt the same lesson in slums of Boston, New York and Los Angeles. Like Macmillan they concluded that the ideologues of Left and Right set higher store by the symmetry of their theories than by the solution of real problems. They believed that the function of government is to combine the best of both worlds – private initiative and public responsibility working together for the common good.

Bobby Kennedy, after his early experiences in office and after his tours of the country as a campaigner, recognized the failure to tackle the problems of the major cities. He saw that it was not a case of throwing money at the problems of poverty. What was needed was an out-pouring of imagination, ingenuity, discipline and hard work. He felt passionately that, in the midst of plenty, poverty is evil. That government belongs wherever evil needs an adversary and when people in distress cannot help themselves. He complained that even as a nation became more aware of the injustice, indeed the danger of serious convulsion in the urban order, that the efforts to right injustice, to open opportunity to build better lives were faltering and slowing down.

He drew attention to the powerful role that free enterprise needs to play in tackling the urban problem. He wanted private enterprise to have the ingenuity to provide decent housing for the 43% of Negroes who lived in sub-standard dwellings. He desired health services for the poor, on a neighbourhood scale, with family physicians who could bring preventive care to the ghettos for the first time. He wanted manpower programmes, not just to create jobs, but to create jobs with possibilities for further education and advancement. He recognized the vital need to involve the community, for they were the ones who had the greatest stake in improving the quality of life. He recognized that welfare wrongly applied would destroy the self-respect and encourage family disintegration.

With his own remarkable initiatives in Bedford Stuyvesan, one of the most poverty stricken areas of New York, he saw the sensible relationship that needed to be established between government and free enterprise. He pointed out that the entire defence establishment included the most secret and sensitive installations and was the best evidence of government and business bringing together the best talents and ingenuity to keep the country strong, vigorous and prosperous. But he pointed out that at that time only 12% of graduating college seniors cared for a career in business or thought that such a career would be worthwhile and satisfying. The reason, he argued, was that the great corporations were seen to play so small a role in the solution of many of the nation's vital problems. Civil rights, poverty, unemployment, health and education – in all of these, business had done far less than might be expected. When the productive assets, machines and plants are owned by private enterprise, when private enterprise is the intricate chain that produces goods and roads to bring food to our tables and clothes to our backs, when private enterprise builds the cities and the industries, creates the jobs, it should have the strength to rebuild centres of poverty, put the people back to work and eradicate divisiveness.

When the Watts district of Los Angeles was burned down in riots it was Bobby Kennedy who gave the correct analysis: 'The Watts riots,' he said, 'were as much a revolt against official indifference, an exposure of frustration at the inability to communicate and participate as they were an uprising about inferior jobs and education and housing. What exploded in Watts is what lies below the surface.'

Race Relations in a Free Society

Race was also in the forefront of the Kennedy mind, the need to let black people share in a free society their priority. They began the struggle to break the white stronghold on the South. The poverty and misery of black America appalled them as much as the discrimination. The American Negro baby had one half as much chance of completing high school as a white baby born in the same place on the same day. The black baby had one-third a chance of completing college, one-third a chance of becoming a professional man, twice as much chance of becoming unemployed. The black had a life expectancy seven years shorter and the prospects of earning half as much as the white equivalent.

These are statistics with relevance today in Birmingham, England, as well as Birmingham, Alabama, to Brixton, London, as well as the Bronx, New York. Again, the promise of the Kennedy years has been dissipated in the years since their deaths.

Bobby Kennedy argued: 'There is a discrimination in New York: Apartheid in South Africa: Serfdom in the mountains of Peru. People starve in the streets of India: Intellectuals go to jail in Russia; Thousands are slaughtered in Indonesia: Wealth is lavished on armaments everywhere. These are differing evils, but they are the common works of man. They reflect the imperfection of human justice, the inadequacy of human compassions: The defectiveness of our sensibility towards the sufferings of our fellows . . . It is not realistic and hardheaded to solve problems and take action unguided by ultimate moral aims and values. It is thoughtless folly. For it ignores the realities of human faith and passion and belief, forces ultimately more powerful than all the calculations of economists or generals . . . Moral courage is a rarer commodity than bravery in battle or great intelligence.

To Revive the Kennedy Spirit
I hope that twenty years after the President's assassination and fifteen after the assassination of his brother your generation will look again at the Kennedy legacy. So much of what was said, so much of what was needed to be done, remains to be said and done. Yours is a generation that has a chance to remedy the mistakes of the past which were so clearly recognized by the Kennedys, but never fulfilled in the aftermath of their deaths.

We need to revive the Kennedy spirit, and this call of Jack Kennedy:

'We know now that freedom is more than the rejection of tyranny, that prosperity is more than an escape from want, that partnership is more than a sharing of power. These are all, above all, great human adventures . . . we are called to a great new mission. It is not a mission of arbitrary power . . . the mission is to create a new social order, founded on liberty and justice, in which men are the masters of their fate, in which states are the servants of their citizens and in which all men and women can share a better life for themselves and their children.'

Your generation has a greater burden of responsibility than any generation that has ever lived. Bobby Kennedy, with a sense of history, recognized the number of the young who had made an impact on the world in the past. He recognized that few of the young have the greatness to bend history. But each can work to change a small portion of events. In the total of all these acts will be writing the history of a generation.

On this sad anniversary of a tragic event, William Manchester, in his new book 'One Brief Shining Moment' has this to say of that terrible day in Dallas: 'The years of grief were ineluctable, yet the time has come to grope for the meaning of that shocking, endless, deeply moving four-day weekend when we each died a little. The President's death was tragic, but his life had been a triumph, and that is how he should be remembered, and celebrated, now.'

Let us remember, and celebrate, by fulfilling the promise of the Kennedy years.

Of all the influences on Peter Walker's political thinking, however, the personality who emerges as having had the greatest impact is undoubtedly Harold Macmillan. Macmillan's writings are a potent inspiration for him. He believes that Macmillan, who was rescued from political obscurity by the emergence of Winston Churchill as Prime Minister, represented the attractive face of the Conservative Party at a time when the Party leadership was complacent and unimaginative. He believes that after the war Macmillan's record as Housing Minister demonstrated what can be achieved by determined leadership, and that his period as Prime Minister was marked by a greater understanding of Britain's domestic and international priorities than has been displayed by any other post-war leader.

Like Macmillan himself, Walker has always dreaded the prospect that Britain should once again experience the economic and social hopelessness of the 1930s. Walker spent the early part of his political life living down the popular perception of the Conservative Party as the party of depression and unemployment, and believes that to allow the conditions of the 1930s to recur is not simply unpatriotic; it is also immensely damaging to the electoral interests of the Conservative Party.

Macmillan's prescription, contained in The Middle Way *always deeply impressed Walker, both as a philosophical definition of modern Conservatism, and as a practical political guide. When therefore, in 1975, Peter Walker was sacked by Margaret Thatcher when she became Leader of the Party,*

Walker, with Harold Macmillan's agreement, began work on a sequel to Macmillan's book entitled The Middle Way – Forty Years On –. *The book had not been completed before the 1979 General Election and still awaits an opportune moment for its publication. Some indication of Walker's thinking in this book was however given when he gave the Iain Macleod Memorial Lecture in 1978 when he spoke to the title 'The Middle Way Forty Years On'.*

In this lecture Walker entered the contemporary argument over the definition of freedom. The new Conservative leadership, attaching great philosophical importance to the concept of the free market, defined freedom as simply the absence of control. Walker believed that if the Conservatives defined their objectives purely in these terms, and denied the balancing and positive role of representative government, there was a real danger that freedom would lose much of its human relevance. He feared the increasingly narrow definition of freedom, and argued that while absence of control was important, freedom as it was understood by the citizen was a much broader concept. This broader, citizen's view of freedom embraced freedom from poverty, freedom from unfair discrimination, freedom from avoidable disease, freedom from ignorance, and freedom from a system of social division which had so limited the ambitions of the young men he had met during his National Service.

IAIN MACLEOD MEMORIAL LECTURE

14 September 1978 The Middle Way Forty Years On

Forty years ago Harold Macmillan wrote a remarkable book called *The Middle Way*. It was inspired by the economic thinking of Keynes, by the appalling conditions that Harold Macmillan had witnessed in the north of England and by the growing threats from the totalitarian right and left.

At the time, Harold Macmillan was a voice in the wilderness, ignored by the Tory leadership when he pointed the way to an economic policy which would end mass unemployment and social misery or when he called for re-armament to meet the growing threat from Nazi Germany. But, twenty years later as Prime Minister, he seized the chance to put into practice so many of the ideas he had dreamed of in 1938. The Macmillan years were marked by economic and social progress at home and enlightened realism abroad. Full employment was given top priority. Housing and social services took great strides forward. With the scars of Stockton still visual in his memory from the 1930s, Britain's regions were given special help. Overseas, the British Empire was dismantled in a way which has earned him lasting credit. And he fought tirelessly for peace in a nuclear world. No wonder we look back on those days as something of a golden age. And it is as well to appreciate the fundamental characteristics of the policies which brought it about: an absence of dogma; a creative relationship between government and industry; efficiency harnessed to the cause of compassion; and an appreciation of Britain's role in the post-war world. As practising politicians we should also note that this approach produced the biggest Tory majority in post-war history.

One of his most successful Ministers – and a close colleague – during this exciting era was, of course, Iain Macleod. Their basic political philosophy was identical. Twenty years ago, when Harold Macmillan was invited to give the CPC lecture at our Party Conference under the title 'The Middle Way Twenty Years After' he said, 'The longer I live and the more I try to read and study the more certain I am that we are heirs to the finest and most enduring tradition in British political thinking.

'We must understand this tradition and we must be worthy of it.

'I believe today as surely as I believed twenty years ago that the only position in politics that we Conservatives can occupy with honour is the middle ground, and the only path in our internal politics that we can tread in triumph is the middle way. I do not say this because I have any special taste or temperament for trimmings. Matters of principle cannot be compromised. But economic and social problems are matters of judgement and practical approach. And indeed the middle of the way approach squares with the most fundamental traditions and habits of man that have been passed down to us from the past as well as with the most urgent needs of the day.

'Conservatives, a national party, the party of national unity whose concern is not to exacerbate or profit from the divisions in society but to heal them, to reconcile them, to balance them, must by its very character and traditions avoid sectional or extremist policies. It must therefore by definition occupy the middle'.

I can see Iain Macleod nodding wisely in agreement even now. And I remember how he echoed Macmillan's words after we lost the 1964 Election, ending thirteen years of Conservative rule: 'I look to the centre,' he said. 'It is the centre which decides elections. For the first time in five elections our grip on the centre has weakened. We must offer something better because we believe in something better'.

Harold Macmillan was a politician moulded by the errors of the pre-war period. Those inter-war years that he described when he said, 'By a strange and terrible paradox we were dogmatic and inflexible in the economic and monetary policies, but weak and without clear purpose in matters of far greater moment and high import. In this mood we were panicked into what was called the policy of appeasement.'

The Middle Way Approach

Harold Macmillan expressed his approach well in *The Middle Way* when he wrote: 'Let us first of all try to discover what it is that people want. That is to say how do they want to live, what are the basic essentials necessary to enable them to live their own lives in their own way. Let us make human liberty the first objective of our plans, that is liberty from humiliation and restraints of unnecessary poverty, liberty from any unnecessary burden of toil, liberty from the haunting fear of uncertainty. This means that instead of working downwards from the realms of abstract theory we shall work upwards from the simple needs of mankind to the complicated economic and social organization necessary to supply those ends. By presenting the case in this way we may be prevented from forgetting that the purpose of economics is to conserve life, to make it fuller, richer and happier and to provide abundant scope and opportunity for human variation'.

Iain Macleod applied these principles to the National Health Service. Not for him any dogmatic hostility because it was a state scheme. His first and over-riding aim was to see that the sick received the treatment that they required. He worked in a similar way at the Department of Employment: he had a deep desire to obtain an atmosphere of industrial unity and to see that full employment remained a permanent feature of our economic scene.

Creative Conservatism

All this is the approach of the practical reformer. It was not enough for Macleod or Macmillan simply to stem the advance of socialism: reaction and a defensive posture had no role in their Tory ideology. Instead, they offered the people an attractive alternative – a free society in which everyone shared its fruits. The Tory Party must always appeal to the people in this way. It must have policies and reforms which the country will support because they are creative, not destructive, designed to improve the quality of everybody's life, not just the privileged few. Macleod expressed this political purpose best as 'the pursuit of excellence' – a pursuit based on an appreciation of human desires and the ideal that everyone had the right to share in excellence, that the best things in life would be available to all. This is essentially the creed of creative Conservatism.

Today, the Macmillan–Macleod philosophy needs to be applied with renewed vigour. Britain is beset with problems – some new, some all too familiar – crying out for radical, practical solutions. The dole queue is back with a vengeance. Inflation is never far away. Our inner cities are marred by social deprivation and decay. Too often have we knocked down today's slums only to build tomorrow's. Racial unrest is growing. And our education system still falls far short of genuine equality of opportunity.

Forty years after Macmillan's 'Middle Way', progressive Tories have a heavy burden to bear: our most urgent task is to reformulate our philosophy and apply it to today's problems. As Conservatives, the keystone of our approach must be individual freedom. But it is now time for progressive Tories to view this concept in a much wider context. It is no longer enough simply for governments to provide a minimum of welfare and a framework of law and order and leave it to individuals to get on with it. Real individual freedom comes when people are in a position to take advantage of Macleod's 'pursuit of excellence'. So we must not be content with freedom under the law. The guiding light in our approach must be a far wider freedom: freedom from Victorian factories; freedom to participate in the industrial decisions which affect our lives; freedom to take advantage of educational opportunities. Only progressive Conservatism can bring these freedoms to everyone.

There is no need to dwell before this audience on how state socialism is inimical to the freedoms I have listed. We must also recognize that the concept of *laissez-faire* free market forces as advocated by the Liberals in the nineteenth century and advocated by a number of economists today also has little in common with real freedom. The unfettered market economy does not help us in the pursuit of excellence because it is only a partial view of freedom. The market economy idolizes people as consumers and, providing the market mechanism is working, it does give consumers a wide freedom of choice. But people are more than just consumers: they are workers, managers, householders, students. Consumer freedom, for them, is only one aspect of a free society and progressive Tories cannot rest easy if governments restrict their activities to oiling the wheels of a market economy. Life is about much more and governments have a role to play in the market place and outside it.

What then are the human needs which the Conservative Party should now recognize forty years after *The Middle Way* was originally written? How can we release the energies and talents of the British people and reverse an age of economic decline? If our guiding light is our broad definition of individual freedom then certain human needs become obvious.

Freedom in the fullest meaning of that word includes the freedom from the humiliation and restraints of poverty; freedom from unfair discrimination; freedom from arduous toil; freedom from the debilitating effects of slum housing.

It means not just prosperity sufficient to provide the basic necessities of food, clothing and shelter, but also sufficient to enable the individual to lead a fuller life, and be able to take advantage of the multitude of benefits and pleasures that the world provides.

It means a concern for the quality of life so that progress is measured not just in GNP or motor cars but in new parks, leisure centres, artistic endeavour – the joy of living.

It means a society in which education is given a new priority and a new role – a perpetual process throughout life and not simply limited to the 5–22-year-old.

It means a society thriving on diversity but undivided by class, race, regional disparities or generation gaps.

These are somewhat higher aspirations than Harold Macmillan would have dared to hold forty years ago. Then the objective of eliminating the malnutrition and poverty of millions of our fellow countrymen dominated everything else. But to achieve these higher aspirations we can still apply the same principles applied by Harold Macmillan and Iain Macleod, best described by both of them in the phrase 'one nation', and described by Lord Woolton, the most successful organizer of an election victory since the war, 'We not only cope but we care'.

Today's Two Nations

In far too many spheres of our national life there are still two nations and not one.

We have two nations within our major cities – the poverty

and the unemployment of the inner city area in contrast to the prosperity of many of the suburbs.

We have two nations in housing where every town and city is divided between the owner occupied estates and the council house estates.

The spirit of two nations still permeates the factory floor. Indeed 'them and us' attitudes have increased rather than decreased in recent years.

We still have two nations in geographical sense with the prosperity of the South-East in sharp contrast to the high unemployment of the North.

We have two nations – one coloured and one white – in many of our urban conurbations where the coloured community has greater unemployment, worse housing conditions and lower educational standards.

And it is this divisiveness, this two-nations spirit, which is threatening law and order in so many of our towns and cities.

The Middle Way to Economic Revival

I want, now to look at some of the practical policies necessary to put these ideals into effect. I believe none is achievable unless Britain has a strong economy. We cannot allow the continuing industrial degeneration of recent years.

We must give a high priority to the creation of a new commercial greatness for it is only out of that new commercial greatness that we can eliminate the poverty, replace the ugliness and patronize generously the arts and culture and leisure so as to provide a better and fuller life. But in doing this we must recognize that efficiency without compassion is self-defeating.

There is a need for a progressive Conservative government to recognize the government role in assessing the national opportunity, in seeing that the free enterprise system is open and just, in protecting the quality of life by recognizing that it cannot tolerate industry creating a bad environment to maximize profits, and by seeing that the cost of removing the scars of pollution must be borne by those who cause them. The Government has a duty to act to rectify the otherwise disastrous consequences of regional imbalance and a Conservative Government has the need to pursue taxation policies and housing policies that enable everyone to have a personal stake in our country.

The Tory Party must be positive in its desire to obtain a true spirit of partnership and participation in industry.

When we strive for participation in industry we are not advancing a new left wing dogma for the Tory Party, we are striving to achieve that ideal of national unity which inspired Disraeli when he wrote *Sybil* over one hundred years ago, that inspired Harold Macmillan in all of the chapters dealing with industrial relations when he wrote *The Middle Way* forty years ago, and that inspired Iain Macleod when as Minister for Employment he said, 'It is madness to think that we can draw up a line of industrial battle in this country and hope that one side or another may at the end of a bitter struggle prove the most powerful'.

Laissez-faire policies encourage that disastrous battle to take place. Socialism welcomes the battle in order to destroy an economic system it dislikes and replace it with a system that wherever it has been tried has proved to be remarkably unsuccessful in creating either human progress or economic happiness. A wit once said that socialism is workable only in heaven where it is not needed and in hell where they already have it.

Socialists frequently batten on to economic discontentment but they are totally unable, indeed unwilling, to emancipate the working class. They are against workers in council houses becoming owner occupiers. They are against workers having freedom of choice for their children in education. To them workers are not just fragments of a block vote at Labour Party Conferences but people whose responsibilities and therefore whose freedoms must be transferred to the politician or the bureaucrat.

The Middle Way for Industry and Employment

We should produce positive programmes in which there is a greater spread of capital and profit sharing becomes a reality in its various forms for the majority of those working in firms and corporations whose activities are based upon the profit motive.

The man who transformed post-war France from decline to revival, President de Gaulle, wrote in his autobiography, 'I had been convinced that modern mechanized society lacks a human incentive to safeguard its equilibrium. A social system which reduces the worker – however respectably paid – to a level of a tool or a cog is, in my opinion, at variance with the nature of our species and indeed with the spirit of sound productivity. Notwithstanding the undoubted benefits which capitalism produces not only for the few but for the community as a whole, the fact remains that it carries within itself the seeds of a gigantic and perennial dissatisfaction. I believed that it was incumbent upon our civilization to construct a new one which would regulate human relations in such a way that everyone would have a direct share in the proceeds of the concern for which he worked, and would enjoy the dignity of being personally responsible for the progress of the collective enterprise on which his own future depended. Would this not be tantamount to the transposition onto the economic plane of what the rights and duties of the citizen represent in the political sphere?'

De Gaulle introduced profit sharing schemes. Prior to his departure from office he desperately wanted to introduce employee participation and he reflected, 'I was to attempt to throw the door wide open to participation in France, an attempt which was to rouse against me the determined opposition of all the vested interests, economic, social, political and journalistic, whether Marxist, liberal or diehard. This coalition, by persuading the majority of the people solemnly to repudiate de Gaulle, was to shatter there and then the possibility of reform at the same time as it shattered my power. Nevertheless, beyond all the ordeals and obstacles, and perhaps beyond the grave, that which is legitimate may one day be legalized, that which is rightful may in the end be proved right.' I hope the Tory Party will reflect upon these wise and thoughtful aspirations of a great political leader.

Advances in technology mean that even if it was acceptable to them it would probably be only available to perhaps 70% or 80%. A society in which 80% were employed and 20% were unemployed would be a society destroyed by friction and divisiveness.

We must also as a party become dedicated to the importance of full employment. There is a crying need for vision in employment. We have lived in a society in which the main objective has been to provide work to human beings from the age of 16–65. I can remember the post-war sensation when union leaders demanded the five day week. That has now been attained. But we no longer have a generation leaving school which will be satisfied by a guarantee that they will be able to work in an unattractive factory, or a mine or even an office for fifty of the remaining fifty-five years of their lives.

We must see to it that capitalism uses technology in such a way that future generations are not obliged to spend a great part of their working hours doing work of little mental or spiritual satisfaction.

Athens without the Slaves

We verge on the lunatic in our approach to economic affairs. We have machines that can replace much of the unsatisfying, dirty and unrewarding work previously carried out by men; we have machines that can produce at greater speed and greater efficiency than in any previous era; we have machines whose parts can be renewed and whose performance can and will be constantly improved. We should rejoice and create a society in which the machine works twenty-four hours a day seven days a week fifty-two weeks a year whilst man toils less and has available to him the time for leisure and pursuits more congenial to human happiness.

Instead we place every restrictive practice upon the machine in order that man may continue a pattern of life heavily committed to unnecessary toil and for many unnecessary poverty.

Unique in history we have the circumstances in which we can create Athens without the slaves. The machine, the computer and the micro-processor are available as the willing, effective and unquestioning slaves. Only the folly of man prevents us from taking advantage of this unprecedented opportunity.

We must apply these healing processes so that all rejoice and benefit from our economic revival.

My vision is an industrial atmosphere in which both the militant shop steward and the unenlightened and dictatorial employer are as extinct as the dinosaur. A new quality of life at the work place, genuine participation and widespread ownership – that is my vision of the middle way in industry.

The Vision for the Middle Way

Let, therefore, the Conservative Party make the 1980s an era where Marx and Adam Smith will be only of historic interest, where creative Conservatism will make unparalleled progress. Let us embark into the decade in which we will for the best part eliminate the divisiveness of bad race relations, eliminate the divisiveness created out of bad housing, provide education as a permanent feature of man's life harness the best in technology and science in such a way as to see that the nation is not divided between the employed and the unemployed but is a nation sharing an ever-fuller life, greater leisure, pleasure and fulfillment.

The middle way is a radical way. It is fired by a vision which once shocked into a sense of fine possibilities in social order cannot walk positively alongside complacency. The middle way is a recognition that society is held together only by the moral bond of mutual obligations; destroy this and society disintegrates in anarchy. The most fundamental of all mutual obligations is the obligation to guarantee to even the humblest the means to live and enjoy a decent life. In my vision of society that is an ethical postulate inherent in the very fact of society. It is not enough that the fruits of society go to the successful even if there is equality of opportunity. In my vision of the middle way everybody has the right to a decent quality of life. Let us in fact move towards a new 'Athens without the slaves'.

I cannot end my speech in better words than those of Iain Macleod when at a party conference prior to a General Election, after outlining a number of themes which the Party should pursue, he said, 'Yet these themes are not enough in themselves. They are but means to the end. Before we meet again in conference we shall be called upon to convince the electorate that we stand for humanity as well as efficiency; for compassion as well as competition; and that for us even the pursuit of excellence is but part of the pursuit of happiness. It is because I believe we can meet this double challenge to heart as well as to head that I long for confrontation at the polls, and when that is behind us I look forward with relish, but with humility, to the chance that our Party will have of placing itself hand and head and heart in the service of our people and of our country'.

That is the atmosphere in which we should enter the coming election battle and that is the way we should start to govern so that in our time we can make great progress upon the journey to which Harold Macmillan and Iain Macleod devoted their lives.

Harold Macmillan's concern about the importance of the middle way, and his recognition of the danger of a retreat into dogma is a favourite theme of Walker's speeches. It was developed with particular reference to his economic thinking when he delivered the Macmillan Lecture to the Young Conservatives in November 1984. He used the opportunity both to underline the danger of the return of high unemployment and to discuss his ideas for promoting economic revival in Britain. Perhaps more than any other recent speech this lecture expressed Walker's controlled anger at Britain's failure in recent years to match his patriotic ideal and his prescription of what was required.

THE MACMILLAN LECTURE TO THE YOUNG CONSERVATIVES

November 1984

No Dogma

Throughout his career Harold Macmillan has spurned dogma: '*Let Sleeping Dogmas Lie*' has been his slogan. In recent years he reflected:

'Economics has now usurped the place held one hundred years ago by theology. The odium economicum has taken the place of the odium theologicum.'

Throughout his life he has refused to allow the high priests of the new theology to distract him from practical matters. When the economic theologians of the 1930s argued that the causes of unemployment lay beyond the power of government to solve, he dismissed their views as '*Economic Calvinism*'.

'Are we to accept economic determination or have we free will? Can we apply human intelligence to make a solution of some of these problems or are they inherent in every system?'

Macmillan belongs to that radical Tory tradition, once described by an american historian as that 'fretful and troublesome company of those whose imagination, having once been shocked into a sense of finer possibilities in social ordering, cannot thereafter walk peaceably alongside complacency.'

The Horror of Unemployment

In Stockton, as he watched the despairing faces of the men who tramped up and down the high streets of Stockton and Thornaby he knew there was no room for complacency. True, there was relief and assistance available, though on a modest scale. But it was not charity, whether from the nation as a whole, or from their neighbours, that these men required. It was work: that was the finer possibility Macmillan struggled to bring them.

Today, the spectre of high unemployment has now returned to Stockton and many other parts of Britain. The labour exchange has become the job centre. National assistance has become supplementary benefit. The dole is better than anybody could have dreamed in the 1930s. Today we are able to cushion the harshest economic hardships of the unemployed. But the social waste is still the same, the human debilitation just as bad. The affront to dignity just as tragic as it was in the 1930s.

Indeed, in some ways, the dangers to our social cohesion are even greater. Some of Britain's blackest unemployments are where the British are black. A generation of black youngsters is growing up, most of whom have never known work. What problems we are storing up for the future. Problems Harold Macmillan recognized.

'The preservation of freedom,' he wrote about half a century ago. 'Is intimately related to economic and social progress. When social evolution slows down the tide of revolution rises. What modern man fails to accomplish by reasoned intelligence and by the voluntary acceptance of inevitable change, other men will seek to achieve by the bludgeon of violence.'

In our struggle to deal with today's mass unemployment, new attention has been drawn to the objectives and prescriptions of the 1944 Employment White Paper. Remember well the first sentence of that document.

'The Government accept as one of their primary aims and responsibilities the maintenance of a high and stable rate of employment.'

The 1944 White Paper was a great triumph for Macmillan for it embodied much of his middle way. What he had campaigned for pre-war became the guideline for all Governments post-war. For a quarter of a century Macmillan's middle way became the basis of British economic policy, a quarter of a century which saw the lowest rates of unemployment, the highest rates of growth and the lowest rates of inflation in our history.

The authors of the 1944 Employment White Paper understood that the key to full employment lay in a flexible and growing economy. Today's generation of policymakers can only ensure full employment in the 1980s and 1990s through economic growth if they face up to the new challenges of international trade and technological advance.

The New Challenges

Let nobody underestimate the scale of these challenges. In international trade we face fast-emerging competitors in the Pacific Basin, South America and South and South-East Asia. But we should not scurry behind protectionist walls to hide from this challenge. If these countries are developing fast we should treat them not as threats to our traditional manufacturing industries, but as great opportunities for British exporters of both manufactured goods and services. Nor should we shrink from high-tech. The Microchip and the information revolution generated by the alliance of the computer with telecommunications should not be seen as a threat to jobs, for it is not, but an opportunity to improve our individual lifestyles and end the drudgery of industrial society. We stand on the brink of better living standards, shorter, more flexible working hours and all manner of new lifestyles. Those societies which have grasped the new technology better than us – such as America and Japan – are those with the fastest falling dole queues.

The key to our success will be our ability to identify and exploit those sections of our economy where we have great natural advantages. We have them in manufacturing as well as service industries and our objective must be to build a balanced economy on the basis of new and expanding industries which are able to hold their own against international competition.

Whenever politicians talk of new industries and international competition they have a great tendency to talk only of the private sector, and of information technology. But we must maintain a manufacturing capacity, just as we have maintained and enhanced an efficient agricultural sector, and we must not forget that Britain is the only manufacturing country in the world which is a net exporter of energy. We have within and around these islands a full range of energy-related activities which can be internationally marketed on a massive scale. We are world leaders in the expertise needed for off-shore oil and gas explorations. We are world leaders in mining technology. We have one of the most sophisticated systems of gas and electricity distribution in the world together with the associated capital goods industries, just at the time when many developing countries are needing to install exactly these types of systems. In food processing and manufacture we have a reputation for quality which will allow us to develop new markets. British agriculture, after all, is the most efficient in Western Europe.

Nor should we write off some of the traditional manufacturing industries which are regarded as permamently at a disadvantage compared with low labour-cost countries, in industries like furniture, textiles and clothing, Britain cannot compete solely on the basis of price, and much of the mass production of these industries has moved permanently to the Pacific Basin. I believe, however, that we can develop a growing market for British goods based on a reputation for quality, and service against which the low-cost countries, remote from the market, will find it difficult to compete.

Look at the revival of Jaguar sales in America, or walk down the best shopping centres of Paris and New York to see quality British goods on sale.

Commercial Revival

National revivals have all been related to recognition of the basic importance of seeing that commercial success is given its true priority. Britain needs a drive in which we will improve all of our commercial and industrial assets: The human asset by means of training programmes and an educational system that recognized the requirements of the future. Far too many of our factories are out-dated, badly arranged, massively wasteful in energy and inappropriate for modern industrial requirements. In machinery we have seen the virtual destruction of the British machine tool industry. British industry *must invest* if it is to succeed.

The infrastructure, too, is in need of renovation, as an

island we need to see that we have the facilities to move goods and merchandise speedily not just throughout our nation but throughout the world.

Government and Industry in Partnership

In all of this we need an enthusiastic collaboration between Government and industry. Let it be recognized that the Three great economic revivals of the past fifty years were achieved by governments believing in free enterprise but recognizing the need for the government to collaborate with free enterprise if it was to succeed. The recovery of the United States under Roosevelt. The revival of Germany under Adenaur, and the transformation of France under the leadership of de Gaulle are the Great Western World examples of government leadership and industrial leadership working as partners together.

The need for Britain to improve its manufacturing performance is clear to see. In twenty years our share of the world market in manufactured goods has virtually halved. Where once the surplus of our manufacturing exports provided us with the money necessary for our imports of food and raw materials, recently we have moved to a substantial deficit in manufactured goods. In 1966 we employed twelve million people in manufacturing. Today we employ four million less. In the same period Japan has increased the number of manufacturing jobs by four million whilst in no way rejecting the new technologies. In the coming decades the great wealth of North Sea oil is going to go down. It would be disastrous if in those decades our wealth from industry and commerce did not go up.

Athens without the Slaves

We shall also need imagination in exploiting the opportunities provided for us by new labour-saving machinery. We live in a society where the traditional objective has been to provide work for human beings from the age of sixteen to sixty-five. Perhaps the next generation will not be satisfied by a guarantee that they would be able to work in an unattractive factory, mine or office for fifty of the remaining fifty-five years of their lives. Perhaps they will see in the new technology the opportunity to emancipate working people from the relentless grind of the production line. Perhaps they will be the first generation who are not obliged to spend the greater part of their working hours doing work of little mental or spiritual satisfaction. When machines can produce at greater speed and with greater efficiency than in any other era, we should embrace the opportunity which that creates with both hands, for now it is the machine which will work twenty-four hours a day, seven days a week, fifty-two weeks of the year, while man is allowed more leisure to pursue his own self-fulfilment. We shall then have truly realized the old dream of Harold Macmillan: Athens without the slaves.

We face great and fundamental changes in our economy, just as we did when Macmillan wrote his middle way. Many are nervous about the implications of these changes for both our economic and social order. The example of Harold Macmillan, however beckons us forward. The changes we now contemplate are no greater than the changes he contemplated in the 1930s and brought about in the 1950s. History holds no comfort for the fainthearted. It is the moral responsibility of politicians to face these challenges and to see that they are met; it is the moral impatience of youth with enquiring minds and optimistic spirits that should be the constant spur to political action.

The Middle Way

Macmillan believed that the free enterprise system produces great benefits for the community as a whole but carries within it the seeds of a gigantic and perennial dissatisfaction. He set out to bring about a degree of order and central direction to the market system, without destroying the individual endeavour and enterprise that is the well spring of that system.

In *The Middle Way* Macmillan wrote:

'There can be no doubt that it is within the power of men to arrange the full employment of their efforts to increase the production of wealth – society has not the right to abandon the individual because, as a result of faulty organization the labour which he is still willing to expend cannot temporarily be utilized.'

Prior to Harold Macmillan's greatest electoral victory in 1959 he said, 'of course we in the Conservative Party do not want to return to the laissez-faire doctrinaire liberalism. Too often that meant the defence not of freedom but of privilege'.

Harold Macmillan posed the question, 'what do these guiding principles, the dignity of man and the consequent necessary limits of political power, the value of our institutions as the cement of society mean in terms of policy?'

He answered, 'moderation should be the keynote of policy, extremes always threaten the family or the individual in one way or another. Too much state control endangers freedom and initiative. But a free for all exalts rights over duties and means that the weak go to the wall. Extremes undermine national unity which is our Conservative Tradition to foster, our aim is to harness different and conflicting interest, not to set them against each other with the strident accents of the class war. We aim to balance them so that all can contribute as one nation to the common good.'

These surely need to remain the aims of our Conservative Party – The one party that has persistently through the centuries sought to UNITE OUR NATION.

When Peter Walker joined Mrs Thatcher's Cabinet in 1979, therefore, his political ideas reflected a range of influences that marked him out from his colleagues around the Cabinet table. From Joseph Chamberlain and Leo Amery he had learned the importance of an international outlook to current affairs and an assertive foreign policy. He had also inherited a distinctive view both of the importance of patriotism, and of its real meaning. The shared experience of the nation which he remembers from wartime London and on which Amery placed so much stress is an important part of his political makeup.

From the Kennedy brothers he had learned the importance

of the appeal to youth. Walker believes that the idealism of young people is an important political resource which politicians should learn to use. He believes that the secret of the political success of the Kennedy brothers was their ability to motivate young people and to harness youthful idealism to a political purpose. In the building of Peter Walker's nation, therefore, he accords a particular place to young people and devotes a considerable part of his political life to encouraging young people to become involved in politics.

Most importantly, from Harold Macmillan Walker had learnt the importance of defining political objectives in terms of people's aspirations, rather than political theory. Walker believes that politicians should not be motivated by preconceived theories; he rejects the dogma of Cambridge as completely as he rejects the dogma of Chicago. He is – as Burke believed that all Conservatives should be – a sceptic. His motivation is a simple desire to build a society in which every citizen takes pride and to which every citizen feels a desire to contribute.

2

Towards a Property-Owning Democracy

While the life of twentieth-century British people changes faster than ever before, British housing policy has become trapped in a well-intentioned, but out-dated, framework. This costs an inordinate amount in public subsidies, while frustrating the wishes of a third of the population living in public sector housing.

There is a growing awareness of the short-comings of council housing, as demonstrated by the government's commitment to allow council tenants to buy their houses. But that policy is insufficient to deal with the problem.

To transfer the ownership of *all* council houses to existing tenants, an idea first put forward by Peter Walker, is the only way out of this impasse. Such a move would improve 'the condition of the people', extend property ownership, cut public expenditure and remove the state from a major area of economic activity. Firstly, the very complexity of the housing market lends strength to belief that the public authorities should withdraw from it as much as possible.

Almost every householder has different requirements for his housing: family size, location, design, personal whim – all play their part. While there are imperfections in the market, there is no evidence that the present policies of general subsidy and local authority control solve these imperfections, except for those who, owing to some disability or handicap, simply cannot cope (and even in this area there is widespread failure).

A market characterized by complexity is exactly the kind best left alone; the inflexibilities of the local authority system result in lack of choice, lack of mobility, ever rising rents and the inefficient use of housing. An ideal system would allow those who can fend for themselves to do so and would provide income-related assistance for those who cannot. Housing for special cases, where people cannot cope on their own, should be considered, financed and administered as a social service.

Rents increase constantly but mortgage payments stay roughly the same and so decline as a percentage of income. Mortgage payments also stop after a number of years thus giving older people much cheaper housing costs; rent never stops. The owner-occupier also ends up with a valuable asset and all the security that brings.

Renting from the local authority is clearly no bargain but few people can pay rent *and* accumulate a deposit; if, however, a mass of lower priced housing came on to the private market, most people would be able to afford owner-occupancy.

It has long been in the interest of the Labour Party to keep a large part of the population as permanent tenants of the government; their rents can be manipulated to electoral advantage and the importance of the government is enhanced by its role as a landlord. There is an assumption implicit in this policy that the public are incapable of deciding their own housing needs.

A financing system in which rent is not related to value but to average cost and in which little or no differential exists between good and bad property creates waiting lists for good properties and substantial dissatisfaction. It eliminates choice at the lower end of the housing market – people do not have a choice between paying more for a new house or less for an old flat – and it does all this while absorbing enormous amounts of public money.

Housing Subsidies

The situation has now reached the absurd stage of providing subsidies for almost everyone. There are 22.2 million dwellings in the United Kingdom: of these 6.2 million are public sector, 13.5 million are owner-occupied and 2.5 million are privately rented.

The approximate subsidy to owner-occupiers via tax relief on mortgage is £4.75 billion. The subsidy to local authority tenants in 1984 consisted of £3.04 billion in central and local government support including £2 billion of Housing Benefit. So the total subsidy to local authority tenants is over £3 billion and total housing subsidies are nearly £8 billion. 6.6 million owner-occupiers receive mortgage tax relief; the total number of dwellings receiving some form of public subsidy is over 12.5 million.

This is not a policy under which the rich subsidize the housing of the poor; it is a policy under which the government collects a sum equivalent to 2.5% of gross domestic product from taxpayers and then pays it back.

One of the results of this is that the really needy do not get all the help they deserve. The public sector is no longer providing a service for the poor and under-privileged alone. Rather it is providing a bureaucratic and highly unsatisfactory service for people who have almost exact counterparts in the private sector. In particular many tenants could buy rather than rent. The argument that most local authority tenants cannot afford to own their own homes just does not bear examination. In 1984 14% of first-time buyers had incomes below £6000 p.a. and 25% had incomes below £7000 p.a. 50% had incomes below £9000 p.a. which was almost the average male wage.

Those who live in council houses are the 'permanent tenantry'; both they and society pay a high social price for this.

The economy suffers from the almost total inability of the council tenant to move freely between local authority areas to change jobs. The council tenant suffers from the lack of freedom to move even within his authority's area to different accommodation more suited to his needs.

Council tenants often feel little need to pay attention to their surroundings, simply because the property does not belong to them. If they were to own their homes, there would be a general improvement in the appearance of what are at present 'Council Estates'. Crime and vandalism would fall.

Council tenants derive no financial benefit from any improvement or repair they make themselves. Not surprisingly, therefore, many tenants allow their houses to deteriorate while waiting long periods for the local authority to arrange for quite simple repairs to be undertaken.

And this condition is self-perpetuity. When they die, they have no property to pass on. Their children are caught in the same trap, forced to live in council housing where they face all the same problems. The remedying of such social problems, even if it involved increased public expenditure on housing, should command a high priority. If it is possible both to tackle these problems *and* to cut public expenditure, then the proposal should command the highest priority.

Public Capital Expenditure on housing (including grants to the private sector) was £3.8 billion in 1984. *Current* subsidies, including Housing Benefit, to the public sector tenants was over £3 billion in 1984. The cost of mortgage tax relief in 1984/85 was £3.5 billion. Total public housing support amounted to £10.3 billion. This amounts to 30% of the total yield of income tax or roughly the equivalent of 9p in the £. We spend an enormous amount on housing.

Look at the contribution made by council house rents to their cost. Rents paid by tenants in 1977 accounted for 42% of the related current expenditure against 65% in 1969. If supplementary benefit is taken into account and deducted from rent income, the net rent receipts in 1977 were £786 million or 27% of expenditure and did not even cover supervisions, management, repairs and maintenance.

In 1984 rent actually paid by tenants amounted to £2044 million or 37.5% of related current expenditure but still did not cover the costs of supervision, management repairs and maintenance.

This means that rent actually paid by tenants made no

contribution at all towards the servicing of the housing debt. In fact there was a deficit of £464 million before any allowance for debt servicing.

Local Authorities' Housing Revenue Accounts

	1969	*1977* (*£ million*)	*1984*
Rent from tenants (including Supplementary Benefit paid as rent, except in 1984)	507	1236	2044
Other income (including rebates/subsidies)	279	1686	3067
Total income	786	2922	5111
Supervision and management	62	364	1017
Repairs and maintenance	117	510	1491
Other current expenditure	12	26	135
Debt service	591	1868	2800
Total expenditure	782	2768	5443

Supervision, management, repairs and maintenance represent the cost of what the local authorities actually do and they are steadily increasing as a proportion of total expenditure. By 1977 they had reached a combined total of 32% of overall expenditure and by 1984 it was 46%. Within this sub-total the cost of repairs and maintenance has risen more slowly. It is the cost of supervision and management that has risen unchecked from 8% of total outgoings in 1969 to 13% in 1977 and to 19% in 1984: this is the administrative cost which a massive transfer of council house ownership would remove.

Total repair and maintenance costs have increased from £117 million in 1969 to £510 million in 1977 and to £1491 million in 1984. Converted to constant 1980 prices these become £468 million in 1969, £779 million in 1977, and £1136 million in 1984, a real increase of 46% in 7 years.

Total supervision and management costs have increased from £62 million in 1969 to £364 million in 1977 and £1017 million in 1984. Converted to constant 1980 prices these become £243 million in 1969, £556 million in 1977, and £770 million in 1984, a real increase of 39% in 7 years.

These costs are rising much faster than rents. It demonstrates the inefficiency and lack of control of expenditure by local authorities. It would be difficult to find many tenants who think they are getting 46% 'more' repairs or 39% 'more' management than in 1977.

What housing authorities are doing now could be done much better privately. Perhaps they were needed when there was a terrible housing shortage after the war. But today the picture is greatly changed. There is a crude surplus of houses. What is needed is renovation of old property and the filling of localized gaps.

Increasing numbers of people want to buy their own homes as every survey of opinion shows. Meanwhile housing authorities continue to pre-empt resources and create a vastly inflated rented sector.

Reform

The Government's Right to Buy policy has resulted in the sale of about 825 000 dwellings at September 1985. This represents about 12% of the stock of public sector buildings in 1979. This is a considerable achievement and has brought about a revolution in terms of property ownership and the condition of some estates. But less than 5% of the dwellings sold have been flats and what has happened is that the better properties have been sold to the wealthier tenants. The policy has not generally helped the old, the poor or those in the worst housing. Current proposals for a substantial increase in the discounts on flats will undoubtedly help but we seem to be getting close to maximum sales.

The policy reduces the overall quality of the public housing stock and this has financial consequences when average repair and maintenance costs rise.

It does nothing to get housing authorities out of housing and will make no real impact on overall housing costs which are unlikely to fall in proportion to the number of houses sold.

A policy of voluntary sales is preferable to no sales at all but falls far short of the sort of radical scheme needed to restore sense and efficiency to the housing market.

The radical policy required is to see that on a specified day the full ownership of all housing authority dwellings should automatically and immediately be transferred to their tenants, subject only to the tenant's obligation to continue paying their rent at its present level until they will have paid rent for a total of 30 years. Analysis of housing authority tenures shows that on this basis:

8% of tenants will pay no more from the start	
10%	for 0–10 years
24%	for 10–20 years
24%	for 20–25 years
34%	for 25–30 years

Effectively the rent payment becomes a mortgage payment and is collected not by the housing authority but by a private institution such as a bank or building society on behalf of the Government. The amount due will be capitalized as a mortgage debt due on the house which will have to be paid off if the house is sold.

The new owners will be responsible for repairs and maintenance from vesting day, subject to an obligation on housing authorities to repair sub-standard property. Thereafter housing authorities will have no role in housing except in special cases (which will be in the nature of social services) for those incapable of managing for themselves.

The transfer would be coupled with an extended Home Improvement Grant system to help the new owners pay for necessary repairs. The residuary obligation imposed on housing authorities would only be in respect of work on multi-unit estates which could not sensibly be done on an individual basis.

General housing subsidies will cease but income-related supplements will be provided through Housing Benefit for those unable to afford their housing payments.

Social Consequences

We would achieve a massive extension of home ownership. As the level of housing satisfaction is much higher among owner-occupiers, this is in itself a great benefit.

Council tenants will no longer be subject to restrictions on repairs, sub-letting, decorating, keeping pets, etc. The atmosphere of conforming on housing estates will be reduced as will the unhealthy social divisions between different estates.

A more efficient use will be made of the housing stock and increased mobility will be facilitated.

Many families who now have no property will have a substantial asset, giving them security, capital and a real stake in the community. There will be a massive shift of personal wealth in favour of a sector of the community which at present has little or none; and this shift will be from the state to the individual. 6.25 million houses at an average of, say, £15 000, will add £93 billion to personal wealth.

People take better care of their own property and more pride in its surroundings and this is noticeable already in areas where a large number of properties have been sold. Vandalism and crime should decrease, thanks to this new pride.

There will be a wide range of choice at the lower end of the housing market allowing people to decide how much they want to spend on housing and to obtain something which suits them. Life will be made much easier for first-time buyers as old properties in bad condition are sold cheaply and then modernized by the purchasers.

Housing authority tenants will no longer be subjected to ever-increasing rents. Mortgage payments will stop for older people, making an enormous difference to their financial well-being. Instead of ever-increasing rents they will have the security of a substantial and appreciating capital asset and the personal satisfaction that goes with home ownership.

Public expenditure costs of supervisions, management, repair and maintenance will cease, but the adoption, of three commitments by the government will involve significant further expenditure:

1 To bring up to standard existing sub-standard property largely through the Home Improvement Grant programme
2 To continue to undertake major maintenance of multi-unit and high-rise developments
3 To continue to assist those who have particular difficulty in fending for themselves

Apart from these three areas, new owner-occupiers will become responsible for repairs and maintenance. In many cases they will do this themselves or for their elderly relatives and there will be relatively little cash expenditure. In the case of multi-unit developments some co-operative arrangement will have to be established.

As the new 30 year mortgages are paid off, so the need for rent rebates and housing benefit will diminish. In future those who rely on this form of assistance will have cheaper houses, so the total cost of such assistance will probably be lower. Provisions for the elderly will certainly be reduced as many of them will have paid off their mortgages.

Three related social issues have attracted regular and trenchant comment from Peter Walker – housing, inner cities and race relations. As a former Secretary of State for the Environment, Walker has considerable personal experience of the complex issues raised in this field. Although it is nearly twenty years since he first addressed the subject he is still outraged by the appalling housing conditions in which some Britons still live, and has often spoken of the sense of rejection experienced by residents of inner city slum areas. He believes that the social tensions caused by bad housing are dangerously exacerbated by poor race relations.

But Walker doesn't simply describe problems he offers solutions. Both his speeches on housing and his record in action have been radical. Between 1970 and 1972 he increased the incentives for housing improvement in areas of high unemployment; the result was a dramatic increase in improvement activity, particularly where depression was deepest. He particularly encouraged those who were trying to organize the restoration of whole inner city areas on a community basis. Jobs were created and housing improved. In recent times he has argued that the precedent should be repeated.

In the mid-1970s Walker was the first senior politician to advocate the transfer of council houses from the Housing Department to their tenants. He believes that this policy represents a welcome redistribution of wealth – from the state to the people – and that, by involving the occupier in management of his own home, it dramatically improves the efficiency of housing provision in Britain. He remains a passionate advocate of this policy, and in 1978 secured the publication of the pamphlet which follows, which sets it out in detail.

There are substantial direct savings to public expenditure of nearly £5.3 billion per annum. Of this the largest element in the termination of local authority house building – about £2.8 billion per annum, in 1984/85. In addition there are the various savings on current expenditure including supervision and management £1017m and repairs and maintenance £1491m.

There will be continuing expenditure arising out of the three commitments mentioned earlier. The first of these (bringing up to standard) is dealt with below but is not something that will continue indefinitely. The second (continuing expenditure on multi-unit developments) is difficult to quantify but an allowance of 30% of current repairs and maintenance costs (£450m at 1984 prices) would seem sufficient.

The third commitment (the obligation to special cases) is not really a housing cost at all but a social service cost. It is equally difficult to quantify but the continuing expenditure on 'special cases' not already provided for by the social services or the voluntary sector should be more than recovered from the savings resulting from the cessation of payments of rebates and benefits to those who become owners outright.

In summary the total saving to the public purse each year would be nearly £5 billion p.a. less the increased cost of Home Improvements Grants.

There will be continuing expenditure on servicing the debt built up by public sector housing. At present this runs at about £2.8 billion per year. In real terms, however, this figure will now fall as inflation erodes its value and the amount of debt outstanding will no longer be increased – indeed actually the reverse.

The opposite table compares the Walker proposal with the present system in the first year

In the first year mortgage payments will make a positive contribution of £1247m to debt service. The gross mortgage payments will decrease over time as more and more tenants will have completed their qualifying 30 years of rent payments

	Present system	*New system*
	(£ million 1984 figures)	
Rents/mortgages	4037	3714*
Rebates	–1993	–1834*
Management	–1017	– 186**
Repairs	–1491	– 447
Other current expenditure	– 135	–
Contribution to debt service	– 599	1247

Present system costs from 1985 National Income Accounts
* Present system less 8% for tenants who have already paid rent 30 years or more
** Management costs estimated at 5% of rents collected

but so will rebates and social security payments. So, of course, will the debt being serviced.

We suggest that these proposals are coupled with an extended Home Improvement Grant programme to enable the new owners to bring their properties up to a reasonable standard. In the case of multi-unit developments the co-operative management structure would have to be able to spend some of this money collectively.

There is the objection that existing owner-occupiers will complain that council house tenants will have an advantage not available to them. In reality they will have the advantage of lower rates and taxes as a result of this scheme. It is suggested that those tenants with a good house will have the advantage over those with inferior accommodation. In reality all will benefit even if the benefit is of differing proportions. It is said that the poor will be locked into their existing housing but in reality they are locked in under the present system whereas their housing may well be renovated and improved under the new scheme.

The reality is that the vast bureaucracy will disappear and the cost of maintenance and repairs when each individual is responsible will be done in a far more cost-effective way than under the present arrangements.

Many ask how do the low income enter the housing market when there are no longer council houses. These proposals will create a new cheap end of the market on a vast scale enabling the new entry to obtain housing on far more advantageous terms than anything that exists at the present time. It will be far cheaper to assist them in their house purchase than to provide them with housing under the present arrangements.

If one calculates the advantages compared with the objections there is a massive advantage for nearly seven million families and the nation as a whole.

The extension of the spread of ownership on this scale would enable there to develop a rented sector including the renting of accommodation which is under-occupied under the present council house arrangements. There will not be less rented accommodation to which people can freely move. There will be more. With multi-storey flats special co-operative arrangements will be required. But only 6.5% of the council housing stock is in blocks over five storeys high and quite a proportion of these blocks have no problems for their occupiers.

The time has come for the positive advantage to be realised and the biggest redistribution of wealth from the state to the people to take place.

THE INNER CITIES

It was in the 1960 Primary Elections in the United States that Peter Walker first recognized the enormous dangers of the deteriorating situation in the inner cities of the Western World. He attempted to tackle this for Britain when Secretary of State for the Environment, and he expressed his views in his book in the 1970s The Ascent of Britain. *Those views are repeated here with updated facts and statistics, which illustrate that the views so vigorously expressed then apply even more today.*

Our Inner Cities

History will judge that the most significant trend of the twentieth century has been the trend towards a world in which the majority of people live in urban areas. At the beginning of the twentieth century only one person in seven lived in a town. By the end the majority of people will be leading an urban life, and the transformation will have come about during a century in which the population of the world will have quadrupled.

At the start of the century the world possessed only eleven cities with a population of more than a million people; within the next few years we will have 300 such cities, and seventeen cities with populations of 10 million or more.

The massive urban conurbations have a new dominance. One-third of the population of Japan live in Tokyo, and one in five of the people of France and Britain live in their capital cities. Within some of these great conurbations there is a new tendency for the inner city to recede. Glasgow and London are two classic examples of cities originally built around industries that are now either disappearing or moving out. It is the middle class who tend to move out with them and the poor and the coloured who move in. Nearly two million middle class people have moved out of New York and nearly two million poor, black Puerto Ricans have moved in. Such a transformation creates impossible conditions for any city, even one that can call upon the resources available to New York; the available resources are no longer sufficient for the growing liabilities.

The city is the most important of our products. It was Winston Churchill who once said: 'We shape our cities and then they shape our way of life.'

Britain's urban problems are aggravated because of the way the majority of our cities developed in the early stages of the Industrial Revolution. These cities contain old housing, old factories and old civic buildings. They have allowed their rivers to become polluted and suffer from a lack of any total concept or vision. The western world faces problems that arise because a society with a disorganized mixture of competing objectives is unable to provide a high quality of life. The several self-interests do not add up to common benefit. It is the way we tackle the problem of improving the quality of city life that will determine whether our cities will prove to be the death or the revival of our civilization.

There are a number of major mistakes we are continuing to make. One of the worst is to allow our cities to spread. It is terrifying that cities in Japan will be 600 miles of unbroken urban sprawl from end to end. Such sprawl has colossal disadvantages; it means that for many of those who live within it travel time to work, play and worship is very much extended and takes up a considerable proportion of that part of life that is available for leisure; it tends to be both ugly and dull; it is inhuman in that it is out of scale with people, and being inhuman it creates an environment in which neuroses, divorce and other social problems tend to increase.

While the deterioration of our inner cities takes place those suffering from it remain relatively silent. One of the worst features of a democracy is that the poor and under-privileged are far less articulate than the wealthy and prosperous. I discovered when I was Secretary of State for the Environment that if there was a project, perhaps the building of a road or a new airport, which adversely affected a middle class area, then petitions were organized, protest meetings took place, there were demands to see the minister, there was publicity in the local and national newspapers, even on the radio and television networks. All this occurred when articulate and informed people felt that their interests were being threatened. When some of our more depressed areas were affected by major schemes of reconstruction, or a road programme, few voices were heard. These people had been accustomed to bad, noisy living conditions and one further blow was not going to make very much difference to the quality of their lives.

Labour Party thinking has been dominated by a paternalism that requires the urban dweller to live in a local authority house and become the permanent tenant of a public authority with a colourless standardization imposed upon him. The same paternalism demands there should be no alternatives in education. It is conformity rather than equality of opportunity that is the main aspiration of the socialist. The dreariness of this aspiration presents the Conservatives with a unique challenge to provide the urban dweller with a far better alternative.

The people who live in the most deprived areas of our major cities have a bad record of voting, perhaps because over the years they have felt that voting for one party or another did not make very much difference. In these areas communications are bad; many of the people do not read widely, they do not listen to news programmes, and they concentrate upon lighter entertainment if they have television. They do not feel they have much power to influence authority, for what complaints they have made in past years have sometimes been listened to but seldom acted upon. The officers of local authorities and government departments appear to them rather remote, both physically and culturally. They have reached a stage of permanent despair in which there is little hope, and as hope disappears tacit acceptance takes its place.

I was not only the first Secretary of State for the Environment in Britain but the first person to hold such a position in any democracy, and I was excited by the possibility of using the resources of a large department to improve radically the condition of our inner city areas. I quickly discovered that the realities of inner city life in Britain were relatively unknown to both local and central government. They knew how many people were on social security in certain localities. They were aware of areas of high unemployment and areas where the crime rate was high. But there were no plans to transform these areas. Primarily, there had been no assessment of what was necessary to improve housing conditions. Certain areas were scheduled for demolition, a process that tended to add to a locality's misery for a considerable period of time. The bulldozer was used not just on houses that needed to be replaced but on countless thousands of houses that could well have been improved and would have provided pleasanter houses than the multi-storey blocks to which their occupants were transferred. There was no accurate information about those people who needed social security and other benefits, and were not obtaining them. There was no basic measure of the horrific conditions that existed or of the quality of life that it was so desperately important to obtain.

I was determined to discover the scope of the problems and then to pursue policies that would transform the reality of today, ghastly and awful as it is for many communities, into a decent and tolerable life in the future.

I decided to examine the underlying problems in the urban areas. Three of these areas were to be complete towns, Sunderland, Rotherham, and Oldham, and three of them districts of major cities which were known to suffer from multiple deprivations, Liverpool, Birmingham and London. I decided that this was not an enquiry that should be in the hands of officials, because I felt that it was important that from the very beginning politicians, and politicians with power, should be immersed in the study. I asked that each of these enquiries be under a steering committee of three people; a minister from my department, the leader of the local council (being the person with most political power in the locality concerned) and a senior partner of a major firm of consultants on urban problems. I took the chair at the enquiry looking into a district of Birmingham. Others of my ministers took the chair at each of the other enquiries. The six leaders of the councils agreed to take their place, and six different firms of consultants were chosen so that we would get a genuine diversity of ideas, observations and solutions from the reports. The store of knowledge thus obtained would enable us to tackle vigorously and competently the problems of our cities.

It is a matter of deep personal regret that within a few months of starting these studies I was moved to another department to become Secretary of State for Trade and Industry. I regret even more that thereafter these studies took a lower priority in the work of the Department of the Environment. Ministerial interest gradually lessened and, when the reports finally appeared, with little publicity or comment, they remained almost totally unknown, not only in the country as a whole but even in the towns and localities upon which the reports were based. Nevertheless they have provided a fund of knowledge for future ministers to draw upon, for they do show the way to future progress, and even more devastatingly they point out the terrible mistakes of the past and the present, demonstrating clearly our continuing failure to provide the resources that are needed.

The Liverpool study covers a district that has all the problems associated with the worst of our inner city areas: the district known as Liverpool 8. Liverpool 8 contains 9.6% of the population of the city but it has a much higher incidence of the worst urban problems. At a time when the city was suffering from an unemployment rate of 8%, Liverpool 8 had a rate of 11% and the worst ward 18%. Whereas 4% of the population of Liverpool are immigrants, Liverpool 8 had 8% and the worst ward 13%. Liverpool 8 had a far greater concentration of families with large numbers of children. In Liverpool as a whole 6% of families have more than four children. In Liverpool 8 the figure is 9%. The number of educationally abnormal children in the worst district of Liverpool 8 is almost twice the figure for Liverpool. The proportion of adults who are mentally ill in the city is 0.5%; in Liverpool 8 it is 2.8%, in the worst ward 4.5%.

The housing conditions in Liverpool 8 are very much worse than in the rest of the city. There are over 1.5 persons to a room in only 3% of the households in Liverpool, but in the worst ward of Liverpool 8 the figure is 9%. In the city as a whole 71% of the population have a bath, an inside toilet and hot water, but only 43% of the people in Liverpool 8 have such fundamental facilities. As to the housing stock in the area, 8% is either due for clearance or has been scheduled as having a short life of only fifteen years or less. Future plans for redevelopment will result in the closure of over 100 of the 180 businesses in the district.

With 9.6% of the total population of Liverpool living in an area of such multi-deprivation, one would anticipate that much more than 9.6% of Liverpool's expenditure would be put into the area. The inner city study discloses the horrifying fact that in this part of Liverpool they do not even obtain the 9.6% of the expenditure which they would get if they were just getting the average allocation for the city as a whole, for they obtain only 6.1% of the money available. The basic principle of the greater the problems the less the effort is, I am afraid, typical of many of Britain's cities.

The first task in tackling our inner city problem is to ascertain the facts. Let us have a look at some of the basic facts concerning four of our major urban areas, the Inner London area, Birmingham, Liverpool and Glasgow.

There are other terrifying facts about these cities. In the Inner London area there are 12 000 children who have been taken from their parents into the care of the local authorities. There are 4000 such children in Birmingham, 2000 in Liverpool and 6000 in Glasgow. The incidence of mental illness in these areas is very high. In the Inner London area, in 1975 alone, 14 000 people were discharged from hospital after being treated for mental illness. The figure was 6200 in

	Inner London	*Birmingham*	*Liverpool*	*Glasgow*
Number of households	1 120 000	360 000	190 000	320 000
Number of households that are council tenants	2 in 7	1 in 3	2 in 5	more than half
Number of households with someone on social security	1 in 6	1 in 4	2 in 5	1 in 4
Number of households with no bathroom	1 in 7	1 in 12	1 in 6	1 in 5
Number of households with no inside toilet	1 in 12	1 in 7	1 in 4	1 in 11
Number of households where there is a one-parent family	1 in 12	1 in 11	1 in 10	1 in 10
Number of households where there is someone suffering from a substantial permanent physical handicap	1 in 18	1 in 19	1 in 12	not available

Birmingham, 3000 in Liverpool. Three-quarters of those discharged will have to continue with treatment. Some of them were discharged against the wishes of their medical advisers.

The crime figures for our cities are bad, and accelerating. In the Inner London area in 1973 one in every 25 children between the ages of ten and sixteen was arrested. This proportion has grown worse since. In 1975 in the Metropolitan Police area young people between the ages of ten and sixteen accounted for half the arrests for burglary and a third of all arrests.

What are the underlying problems that create these conditions? There is the growing problem of unemployment, a problem that increases as our public transport system breaks down. Many lower income families living in inner city areas are unable to provide their own transport, and as public transport ceases to function they become immobile. A second problem is the crime rate itself, for not only is it increasing and self-reinforcing but it creates further problems which encourage delinquency.

It is very difficult to attract new businesses to the area of high crime rate in Birmingham and Liverpool. Businesses that are perpetually burgled and have to have windows barricaded find other locations. More people become unemployed and the crime rate rises. This particularly affects young people.

These are the areas with the oldest school buildings and the most difficult children, a combination which makes it much more difficult to attract good teaching staff. And even if they had the best teaching staff available the children would still return to deplorable housing conditions. The truancy rate in these districts is very high. In the Inner London area the truth is constantly concealed by the authorities: these are the areas with the highest levels of illiteracy, which makes communication much more difficult.

These districts contain a large proportion of elderly people who have nowhere else to move to and are trapped in the locality. They are the reception areas for those who move to our bigger cities, be it from Glasgow, Cork or Bombay. They are areas where there is very little proper professional advice available. The best solicitors do not site their offices in such localities, so the quality of legal advice is inferior. Doctors prefer to live and work in pleasant areas rather than where their professional skills are most needed.

Fundamental to the improvement of life in our inner cities is the task of creating better job opportunities. A combination of high unemployment and low earnings brings about a rapid deterioration in the quality of life in these areas. As jobs become scarce, longer journeys are needed to obtain work, and as public transport breaks down job opportunities are reduced. As the price of public transport increases the expenses of travelling considerable distances become a factor in still further reducing living standards. The necessity for mothers to work longer to supplement the family income means that the children receive less attention and the likelihood that children will play truant and commit petty crimes is correspondingly increased. The prospects of employment and good earnings are worse for the unskilled than the skilled, worse for black than white, worse for the school-leaver than those already established in their jobs. The inner city areas contain predominantly the unskilled and the blacks, and they also have a very substantial volume of school-leavers in proportion to their total populations. The difference between the aspirations and the qualifications of many of the younger people represents a basis for discontent.

I conclude that the only method of tackling the inner city problem is the creation of an inner city authority that can bring a total approach to the problem.

I would give the Department of the Environment the power to designate an inner city district as a development district and for a period of time give a development corporation the resources and the powers to bring that district up to the national average.

We can measure the average quality of housing, employment, education, social services. We can measure by a house-to-house survey the position that exists in the designated inner city district.

It would be the task of the development corporation to pursue a programme which, perhaps over ten to fifteen years, would improve the position within the development district so that it swiftly reached the national average.

There would be no difficulty in recruiting the people to manage the executive side of the development corporations because they would be given one of the most satisfying opportunities for applying their managerial skills. There would be no difficulty in obtaining talented personalities who would give vision, energy and enthusiasm to the project. The financial resources allocated by government would reach those people who needed assistance. The development corporation could harness a great deal of inward investment from the private sector with appropriate inducements, both financial and in location.

As Secretary of State for the Environment I decided, when confronted with the unique development of the docklands, that this could only be managed by a new authority and would not be managed by a range of local authorities, some of whom had so dismally failed in rebuilding and restructuring the areas after the extensive bomb damage in the last war. I am delighted that Michael Heseltine, when Secretary of State for the Environment, implemented this concept.

Michael Heseltine, with his knowledge of the Docklands development and his knowledge of the inner city problems, has also reached the conclusion that these problem areas will only cease to be problems if the administrative machine is created for a total approach to be applied. Had that total approach been organized a decade ago, considerable progress would have been made in eradicating the problems of the inner city areas.

The problem of our inner cities is caused by the concentration of people living on the economic and social margins of society. This concentration is increasing. The economic and social conditions are deteriorating. The problem of the inner city is the most serious social problem facing the British Government.

The cost of failure to solve the problems of our inner cities will be paid in lives of misery for many of the inhabitants. The reward of well thought out dynamic solutions could be cities of beauty and opportunity where men and women can decide for themselves how they will work, live and enjoy their leisure. This is a reward of such magnitude that it should command the highest priority in any political party.

RACE RELATIONS

Deeply associated with better housing and the inner cities problem has been the problem of race relations. Peter Walker has always had a passionate hostility to racial prejudice – a hostility derived from strongly held religious beliefs. At a political level, Walker sees racial conflict and resentment as a problem of alienation and intolerance, exacerbated by an inability to understand and address areas of friction. In his public life Walker has made the creation of a society where racial tension is dealt with confidently and sensitively one of his political imperatives.

In many speeches Peter Walker has expressed his fears of our becoming a nation divided, where a young West Indian might be less privileged than the young white, despite their common British nationality and despite both of them having, in theory, the ability to enjoy all of the opportunities available to citizens of this country.

For Walker it is important that the citizens of Africa, Asia and South America admire a Briton for coming from a country which in practice, not just constitutional theory or mouthed religion, recognizes the dignity of an individual irrespective of race, religion or colour. It is not always convenient for Conservative politicians, particularly those from rural Midlands constituencies, to think such thoughts – and less so to take positive action on them. But the issue of racial suspicion did confront Walker in his own constituency of Worcester. When there was a considerable outcry against a planning application for the building of a mosque for the minority Asian population who had come to Worcester, it was Peter Walker, against the wishes of many of the local Tory councillors and personalities, who argued that they should be allowed to have their place of prayer.

In private life he has organized training in the building industry for groups of young West Indians living in the Brixton area, and he also promoted a scheme encouraging the participation of young West Indians into the 'enterprise economy'.

Race relations is more than an issue to be aired and pontificated on. Peter Walker believes that crucial to gaining the confidence in British society many coloured families lack, is politicians acting personally on their behalf, to the direct benefit of them and their families.

His views were passionately put when he spoke at Interfaith and All-Party Rally for Racial Justice at Central Hall, Westminster.

I approach the issue of race relations as an individual who like Lord Randolph Churchill, when asked in South Africa to what race he belonged, replied, 'human'. I approach it as a politician who believes in the importance of stability and believes that stability can only be achieved by unity, by creating the vision of one nation devoid of friction which was the concept of Disraeli. In the nineteenth century he saw the dangers of two nations – one rich and one poor. In Britain today we still have the dangers connected with poverty. We now have the added ingredient of two nations – one white and one coloured. In my view the greatest danger to society is the alienation of a class or a race from government. All our citizens, irrespective of colour, must be welcomed as full citizens of the United Kingdom not only in the negative sense of non-discrimination but in the positive sense of enjoying with all the other citizens the improvement of our social conditions. Lord Milner once defined patriotism as the desire to see that every citizen born rejoiced in his birthright of being born British. We have much to do before that objective of patriotism is attained. True patriotism does not divide. It unites all our citizens and that is what I believe my party should stand for.

It was fourteen years ago that Martin Luther King wrote to his fellow clergymen from a jail in Birmingham, Alabama. He wrote because the church had issued a statement describing his activities as unwise and untimely. Perhaps at this rally we should again contemplate the words that that Christian and that fighter for racial equality wrote with all of the benefits of the time to meditate in jail. He wrote:

> 'I had also hoped that the white moderate would reject the myth concerning time in relation to the struggle for freedom. I have just received a letter from a white brother in Texas. He writes: "All Christians know that

the coloured people will receive equal rights eventually, but it is possible that you are in too great a religious hurry. It has taken Christianity almost two thousand years to accomplish what it has. The teachings of Christ take time to come to earth." Such an attitude stems from a tragic misconception of time, from the strangely irrational notion that there is something in the very flow of time that will inevitably cure all ills. Actually, time itself is neutral; it can be used either destructively or constructively. More and more I feel that the people of ill will have used time much more effectively than have the people of good will. We will have to repent in this generation not merely for the hateful words and actions of the bad people, but for the appalling silence of the good people. Human progress never rolls in on wheels of inevitability: it comes through the tireless efforts of men willing to be co-workers with God and without this hard work time itself becomes an ally of the forces of stagnation. We must use time creatively, in the knowledge that the time is always ripe to do right. Now is the time to make real the promise of democracy and transform our pending national elegy into a creative psalm of brotherhood. Now is the time to lift our national policy from the quicksand of racial injustice to the solid rock of human dignity.'

Later in that letter he said:

'I have watched the white churchmen stand on the sideline and mouth pious irrelevancies and sanctimonious trivialities. In the midst of a mighty struggle to rid our nation of racial and economic injustice, I have heard many ministers say: "Those are social issues with which the gospel has no real concern." And I have watched many churches commit themselves to a completely otherworldly religion which makes a strange, un-Biblical distinction between body and soul, between the sacred and the secular.

'I have travelled the length and breadth of Alabama,

Mississippi, and all the other southern states. On sweltering summer days and crisp autumn mornings I have looked at the South's beautiful churches with their lofty spires pointing heavenward. I have beheld the impressive outlines of her massive religious-education buildings. Over and over I have found myself asking: "What kind of people worship here? Who is their God? Where were their voices when Governor Wallace gave a clarion call for defiance and hatred? Where were their voices of support when bruised and weary Negro men and women decided to rise from the dark dungeons of complacency to the bright hills of creative protest?"

'Yes, these questions are still in my mind. In deep disappointment I have wept over the laxity of the church. But be assured that my tears have been tears of love. Yes, I love the church. How could I do otherwise? I am in the rather unique position of being the son, the grandson, and the great-grandson of preachers. Yes, I see the church as the body of Christ. But, oh! How we have blemished and scarred that body through social neglect and through fear of being nonconformists.'

Perhaps we should wonder what kind of people worship in our churches and the degree to which they genuinely wish to overcome racial discrimination and racial prejudice. Perhaps we should ask why are so many voices silent against not only the utterances of extreme and repugnant organizations like the National Front, but also against the utterances of many ordinary people who out of either unjustified fear or lack of constructive convictions mouth the phrases of prejudice.

In the early 1960s I saw the tragedies of racial prejudice in America. I saw the district of Watts in Los Angeles the day after it had been burned down. I travelled through those areas of New York that have become 'no-go' areas for the police. I saw the misery of the almost unlimited crime in districts not far from the White House itself. I was determined to see that no such mistakes were made in Britain. Alas, my determination and the determination of others has not been enough and there is much evidence that with a coloured population of only 3% of our total we are failing to establish genuine equality of opportunity and good race relations here in Britain.

We are creating what could be a lost generation of underprivileged, semi-literate and unemployed black youngsters. Many of them are fast being lost to the borstals, prisons and psychiatric units. For many of them their grievances are so deep-set there is little we will be able to do to remedy the vicious attitudes that we have been responsible for developing in them.

Their bad housing, bad education and high unemployment is of such dimensions that unless tackled effectively and quickly it will bring to Britain the crime, the bitterness and resentfulness that has been such a tragic feature of American cities that equally failed to identify the aspirations, hopes and deep disappointments of their coloured population.

The current realities of the coloured population in Britain are frightening. If you are a West Indian there is six times the chance you will be sharing accommodation with another family than if you are not West Indian. The proportion of West Indian families living in what is officially described as 'overcrowded conditions' is ten-fold the proportion of the country as a whole. I believe there are districts in some of our inner city areas where of the late teenagers one in five could now be defined as homeless.

Whilst unemployment in this country has doubled, unemployment for the coloured population has quadrupled. There are many districts where well over half of the teenage coloured young are not only without a job but know that their chances of getting a job are more than three times worse than the white teenager.

We have an urgent task of dissolving the new ghettos in which many coloured families are living: the physical ghettos in our inner city areas: physical ghettos that contain both white and black, both in equal need of action to rescue them and their children, and perhaps as Bobby Kennedy once put it 'Particularly the ghettos of the mind which separate white from black with hatred and ignorance, fear and mistrust'.

We must take action to end neighbourhoods of poverty in the midst of oceans of material prosperity. Wealth is conspicuous but poverty hides, but it is in the hide-outs of poverty that social disorder and disunity is created.

We have in Britain an unparalleled opportunity for success. We have a long history of tolerance and compassion and respect for the rule of law. We have genuinely democratic institutions. What we need is a period of determined and positive action. The action is more difficult and needs more courage because without doubt prejudice is widespread. To some extent it is a repeat of the age-old struggle – the roar of the crowd on one side and the voice of your conscience on the other.

To succeed will not only have enormous implications here in Britain but immensely important implications overseas. This is the first time in history when those countries where the majority of the population are coloured are within hours and not weeks of each other. This is the first time in history when the white nations of the western world and the nations of Africa and of Asia are going to depend on each other for raw materials, for markets, for development of technology and for the application of education. Unless we can create a spirit of collaboration and friendship differences of race and racial attitudes may well become the greatest threat to world peace. As Adlai Stevenson said, 'On this shrunken globe men can no longer live as strangers. Our prayer is that men everywhere will learn finally to live as brothers, to respect each others differences, to heal each others wounds, to permit each others' progress and to benefit from each others' knowledge'.

Here in Britain we could set an example to the world in achieving that objective.

Perhaps the most famous phrases of Martin Luther King were those in his Lincoln Memorial Lecture when he said:

> 'I have a dream today. I have a dream that one day down in Alabama with its vicious racists, one day right there in Alabama little black boys and little black girls will be able to join hands with little white boys and little white girls as brothers and sisters. I have a dream that one day even the state of Mississippi, even a state sweltering with the heat of injustice, sweltering with the heat of oppression, will be transformed into an oasis of freedom and justice. I have a dream that my four little children will one day live in a nation where they will not be judged by the colour of their skin but by the content of their character.'

I have similar dreams for relationships here in Britain. But to dream is not enough. I have a plan, a plan that I believe we must apply today and in the years ahead so that we do succeed where other nations have failed. It is not a plan based upon changing the law or trying by legal methods to end racial discrimination because racial discrimination can only end in the hearts of men and is only meaningful when black, brown and white have a genuine equality of opportunity. It is no use creating a situation in which we can boast that the black has a mouthful of legal rights but an empty stomach and is living in a hovel.

It is a plan in which we will provide the resources to see that in housing, in education and in employment there is equality of opportunity for all of our citizens irrespective of colour; a plan to move into the inner city areas where many of our coloured population are living and many of our poorest white citizens are struggling with them, and to provide them with housing equal in standards to that of the country as a whole, and to provide them with educational facilities and the industrial training facilities that will give them a new opportunity; to provide them with employment opportunities that will end the character-destroying permanent unemployment which currently is their lot.

But these are plans for governments and local authorities. Plans in which politicians have to be determined and have to recognize the totality of their task. But that plan is not enough for it leaves out an essential human ingredient. I have a plan for our churches. I believe, for example, there are probably something like 80 000 West Indian households where either unemployment or bad housing has brought despair. Are not our churches of all denominations strong enough and powerful enough to identify such families and to give them friendship, understanding, help and guidance?

Is this not a time when everybody who claims to be a Christian individually takes on the responsibility of eradicating the prejudice that exists and replaces it with kindness and with friendship? Should not Christian businessmen see that they are making a contribution to develop the skills and talents of the younger coloured population? Should not each family as neighbours be good neighbours to their coloured friends? Should not the churches see that instead of prejudice on the problems of race relations they actually establish good race relations?

I hope that my children will live in a world where racial prejudice is but a matter of historic interest. But if that hope and Christian position is to be reached it requires the dedicated service not just of politicians and of governments but of each of us as individuals.

In 1976 Walker expressed his horror as to what was emerging in a letter to the then Prime Minister, Mr Callaghan. The letter made considerable impact. It was published in full in a number of major newspapers and in the political weeklies. The reply from the Labour Government was, however, disappointing. The letter illustrates the degree that Peter Walker has always felt that in Britain there was a unique opportunity to demonstrate to the rest of the world how harmonious and successful racial relations could be achieved. He felt that the total size of the problem was one that government, local government, commerce and industry were, if organized, able to tackle. And yet what tended to occur was a great deal of rhetoric, legislation to prevent acts of positive hostile discrimination but none of the resources of housing and education, and job opportunities that were needed if the problem was to be resolved.

From: The Rt. Hon. Peter Walker, MBE, MP
House of Commons

15th June 1976

Dear Prime Minister,

Because for the last two years I have made an in-depth study of the problems of our West Indian community I would have written this letter to you irrespective of the events in Southall. These events have highlighted the anguish and problems of our Asian community, particularly the frustrations of the younger generation of Asians. But while the Asian community have immense problems of housing, employment and education, they are problems that are not as grave or as extreme as those currently being suffered by the 120 000 households of West Indian descent

When I enjoyed the privilege of being Secretary of State for the Environment I was deeply concerned that there were concentrated in a number of our inner city areas a coloured population suffering from considerable multi-deprivation.

A combination of bad housing, bad education and racial prejudice meant that they were destined to be the unemployed and the perpetual poor.

The true facts were not available and to obtain the facts was one of the purposes of my instigating the three Inner City Studies in Liverpool, Birmingham and London – all three in districts with a substantial immigrant population.

Although during my period as Secretary of State for Trade and Industry there was relative full employment it was clear from my observations as the Head of that Department that our coloured minority were not enjoying anything like the opportunities that were available to the country as a whole.

The reality of their bad housing, bad education and high unemployment is of such dimensions that unless tackled effectively and quickly it will bring to Britain the crime and bitterness and the resentfulness that has been such a tragic feature of the American cities that equally failed to identify the aspirations, hopes and deep disappointments of their coloured population.

London and Birmingham possess the main concentration of West Indians. Our first and second biggest cities are therefore threatened unless we succeed in taking effective and imaginative action.

During these two years I have spoken to social workers clergymen, industrialists, policemen and West Indians (both young and old) in some of the districts in which the West Indian population is concentrated. I want you to know about the facts of the present situation.

A very high proportion of the West Indian population are young children and teenagers. Alas, the proportion of one-parent West Indian families is half as much again as the proportion of our population as a whole. With this background housing is, of course, fundamental.

Housing

I remember the horror with which, within a few weeks of becoming a Minister, I talked to one West Indian family – husband, wife and four children – who were living in one room in Brixton without a single window to that room. I was determined to see that such conditions ended. They have not. They are getting worse.

If you are a West Indian there is six times the chance that you will be sharing accommodation with another family than if you are not West Indian.

West Indians have two-thirds again more people per room than the population as a whole.

The proportion of West Indian families living in what is officially described as overcrowded conditions is tenfold the proportion of the country as a whole.

In London it has been shown that not only have the

West Indians obtained about half of the proportion of council houses that their population warrants, but they have also been allocated housing in what tend to be the worst and oldest estates. In the enquiries I have made it is certain that their lack of articulation has resulted in them obtaining but a small proportion of the rent allowances and rent rebates to which they are entitled. Nor are they aware of the statutory rights that are available to them in the sphere of housing. Of all groups in our country there can be none who are suffering from more overcrowded conditions and who are deprived of what we consider to be the basic standards of housing. Of the late teenagers in certain districts I believe there are as many as one in five who could not be defined as homeless.

Education

Being concentrated as they are in our worst inner city areas the majority of West Indian children are in old schools. The turnover of teachers is massive. You will find few teachers in any of the schools in which they are concentrated who have been there for five years. Some of the children have as many as three or four different teachers in one year.

A high proportion of West Indian children are leaving school with totally inadequate standards of literacy and numeracy to the deep disappointment of their parents.

It is not surprising that with the fast turnover of teachers and the fact that 74% of West Indian women of working age are out at work that the truancy rate is of massive proportions and in many cases the teachers are relieved when some of their more difficult pupils are absent. Far too many young West Indians from the age of 12 and 13 onwards are leaving school to join the homeless and the unemployed, living on cash earnings and sometimes on crime.

As yet these increasing groups of unemployed and homeless teenagers have not been mobilized for political or criminal purposes on any scale but if they are the effects could be massive in both London and Birmingham – effects that have only previously been seen in the worst inner city areas of America.

Unemployment

The 1971 survey showed that of the West Indian unemployed only two-thirds registered. From the enquiries I have recently made in both Birmingham and London I believe this is still the position, particularly amongst teenagers. The boy who has played truant from school tends not to sign on for unemployment.

From 1974–76 unemployment in Britain doubled, but for the West Indians it nearly quadrupled.

In February 1976 there were more than 16 500 West Indians registered as unemployed. I believe in reality there were nearly 25 000 unemployed – one for every five West Indian households, the majority of them teenagers. In some districts you will find nearly half of the West Indian teenagers without a job and those with a job have had to make three times as many applications for a job as their white counterparts of identical educational achievement.

The history of cities has shown that irrespective of being black or white high unemployment among teenagers has always meant a massive increase in crime. You will know as a former Home Secretary how the present crime rate amongst West Indians has dramatically increased. We are in danger of losing a substantial proportion of a whole generation of young West Indians to prisons, borstals and psychiatric units. We are bound to pay a heavy price if a generation of young people is lost in this way. The realities of the West Indian young is that they are frequently badly educated. They have little motivation; no skills; they are homeless; they are devoid of guidance and more and more devoid of hope. In such conditions they are increasingly becoming positively hostile to the white population and particularly to white authority.

Of 120 000 West Indian households I believe that two-thirds of them are either badly housed or suffering from unemployment and the majority of them have a much lower standard of literacy and numeracy than the nation as a whole. There are probably, therefore, 80 000 West Indian households in urgent need of a change for the better if they are to have anything like the equality of opportunity that the rest of the country enjoys.

We have districts in which in every street there are West Indian families in overcrowded and deploration housing conditions. Every other teenager is unemployed or playing truant from school; low incomes and numerous one-parent families; and above all, no hope. This situation must be ended.

To fail will mean not just the continuation of the misery of large numbers of the coloured population in Britain. To fail will also bring increasing misery for the white indigenous population living in our cities. For to fail will mean an increase in crime. Failure will bring increased burdens on the social services. Failure will mean deteriorating industrial relations. To fail when the task is relatively so small will show a nation incapable of tackling a problem, the details of which are known and the solutions for which are readily available.

Successive governments, including your own, have operated in Britain general improvement areas, the priority neighbourhood schemes, the housing action areas, the educational priority areas, the urban aid programme, the job creation programme, the youth employment scheme and the community industry scheme. And yet I must tell you that the help is not reaching this group of people who need it most. During the operation of all of these schemes their unemployment has increased, their housing conditions have got worse, the crime rate has soared to new heights, and we are making no substantial break-through as far as education is concerned.

It is vital for you to discover immediately why it is

that with all of these schemes available so little is being achieved. The Inner City Report on Liverpool had disclosed the startling fact that the district of Liverpool that has double the proportion of immigrants as the City as a whole has 50% more of the larger families, has nearly double the crime rate, and treble the overcrowding, is the district that contains 9.6% of the population of Liverpool but receives only 6.1% of the local public expenditure of Liverpool.

This is why I urge you, as Prime Minister, to call together those Cabinet Ministers who have responsibility in these spheres – the Secretary of State for Employment, for Education, for the Social Services, and for the Environment – to demand of them that they first of all ascertain quickly the reality of the dimensions of the problems facing our West Indian community and then to see that, in collaboration with the local authorities primarily concerned, a system of management is put into operation whereby the resources that are meant to be available to these people are made available to them.

There is no doubt that with determination within five years we can by positive action bring an end to the misery for this population and to bring them somewhere near to an equality of opportunity with the rest of the nation as a whole.

It is no use talking of lack of racial discrimination in this country if a lack of positive action means that the worst housing, the worst jobs – or no jobs – tend to be concentrated upon one community.

There is no reason why with an imaginative five year programme positively managed that at the end of that five years the housing, educational training and the job opportunity standards for the West Indians are at least equal to those of the rest of the population. Eventually this action will have to be taken. The question is will it be done after racial relations have deteriorated still further, hatred has been built up in the hearts of the

West Indian community, hostility has been created by the white community's resentment of the crime and the property damage that will have been attributed to the coloured community? Britain has a size of problem that is manageable. Britain does have the resources to manage it. I plead with you as Prime Minister to take the urgent action that is now necessary.

Yours sincerely,
Peter Walker

The Rt Hon. James Callaghan MP,
The Prime Minister,
10 Downing Street,
London, S.W.1

Peter Walker recently said in a speech at Cambridge, 'I am deeply depressed that positive and practical measures were not taken in the early years and that the position has deteriorated considerably as a result of the world recession. When it came to the recession it was frequently the untrained black who was first to be made unemployed. The substantial increase in their unemployment brought a large increase in crime rates in the districts in which they live and the substantial increase in the crime rate has eradicated many of the existing businesses that operated in those districts. Like a spiral the unemployment became still worse. In recent years in a number of inner city regions drug peddling has become a main feature. Riots have been organized and taken place.

We must retain our determination to see that the far deeper social and economic problems that exist now are tackled so that the deterioration ends and the recovery begins. Britain must give a lead to the world in the achievement of the eradication of racial prejudice.

3

The Coal Dispute

The great coal strike of 1984/85 was the most serious peacetime political threat to British democracy in living memory. Peter Walker was the Minister responsible for conducting Government policy throughout that long, gruelling dispute. In this essay written for the West Midlands Conservative Association he gives his account of the political background to the dispute and how a united Tory cabinet met the threat to democracy by the Marxist Left. The coal strike required grit and determination to fight. But it also gave Walker the chance to put into practice his long-standing belief that, for a society to succeed, it must struggle to find the right balance between efficiency and compassion.

When the Conservatives won the June 1983 election I had no particular expectations. There are few people who remain Minister of Agriculture for an entire Parliament, let alone two. I was a wet. I could have been moved to another department, or dropped altogether.

When Mrs Thatcher called me the morning after the election, she kindly paid tribute to my work at Agriculture. She then explained that she wished me to move to the Department of Energy, a small department which had been but a division of the Department of Trade and Industry of which I had been Secretary of State in the later half of the Heath Government ten years before. But it was about to take on a new significance. During the next Parliament, she said, the Government could be challenged by Arthur Scargill. He would use the industrial clout of the miners to achieve his Marxist objectives.

She said that if that did happen she felt there would be

no one more experienced or better at communicating the Government's case. I accepted the responsibility.

I had been involved in the coal dispute of 1973/74. But that was with a union led by Joe Gormley, who had tried to deliver a settlement without a strike. It was a strike in which the miners had been balloted. It was a strike in which there was no mass picketing, and none of Scargill's Marxist militancy.

I made a careful study of my potential opponent, a fascinating exercise. I studied not just press cuttings but also the leaflets he had published, the press statements he had issued, and the individuals and countries with which he was connected. My study portrayed a man dedicated to Marxism, and one prepared to use the industrial muscle of his union to impose his Marxist agenda.

One pamphlet he had produced (with another Marxist, Peggy Kahn, who for several years worked closely with him) attacked the proposals put forward by the Labour Government and the TUC to improve employee participation and introduce worker directors. Scargill's approach was simple. He was against employee participation lest it make capitalism more attractive to the workers. The important thing for Scargill was to generate total hostility to a capitalist and liberal democracy.

Scargill was a frequent visitor to the Soviet Union. He had a close association with Eastern Europe's totalitarian regimes. And he was friendly with the Communist-controlled unions of Western Europe.

But he faced a major hurdle: the democratic tradition of his union. The NUM had always balloted before industrial action took place, with the votes counted by an independent organization. So my aim was clear: to pursue policies towards the coal industry which would be good for that industry, good for Britain and which would create the conditions which would make it impossible for Scargill to win a strike ballot.

Some industrial correspondents and many left-wing politicians have argued that the Government provoked the strike to defeat Arthur Scargill. Nothing is further from the truth.

My advice to the Prime Minister was to pursue policies that would prevent Scargill from ever being able to win enough votes for a strike. The Prime Minister totally supported that strategy.

On three occasions Scargill had already balloted for a strike and failed. I did not believe that the National Union of Mineworkers would allow him to take strike action without a ballot. They never had.

I was wrong. There was major industrial action without a ballot. A large number of miners came out on strike, many because of intimidation. But the policies we pursued made Scargill frightened of balloting for a national strike because he knew he would lose the vote again. That put him at a grave tactical disadvantage. It meant that one-third of Britain's miners remained at work and many of the other two-thirds remained resentful of the way Arthur Scargill had bulldozed them into the strike.

The economics of coal were never really in dispute. There were twenty or so pits which were hopelessly uneconomic. They were pushing up the price of coal and doing real damage to the industry's long-term prospects.

I was determined to see that the closures took place in such a compassionate and generous way that the miners would not follow Scargill to the barricades. I was confident the miners could be convinced that it was in their long-term interest that substantial investment went into the good pits and that British coal became more competitive, both at home and abroad.

I went to the Cabinet with proposals to guarantee no compulsory redundancies and, for those who wished to go for early retirement, payments and pensions more generous than anything ever seen before in Britain.

For younger miners there would be voluntary redundancy with substantial payments so that they could make a new start elsewhere. The cost was enormous. But the Government accepted my proposals – hardly the action of a government which was seeking a strike.

I inherited as Chairman of the National Coal Board, Ian

MacGregor, an American banker with a distinguished record as an industrial leader and a lifelong association with the coal industry. He had been chosen by my predecessor, Nigel Lawson, who persuaded him to switch from the chairmanship of British Steel to take on the National Coal Board.

I understand it had been originally envisaged that Sir Robert Haslam, now the new Chairman of the National Coal Board, would have been given the task, and indeed he wanted it. But Sir Robert had been ill and it may have been this that deterred Nigel Lawson from appointing him.

I was favourably impressed by Ian MacGregor. I agreed with his assessment of the coal industry. Everyone knew that there were pits that needed to be closed, that productivity needed to be improved, that the top management needed to be tightened and that change needed to come about in a civilized and compassionate way.

Ian MacGregor appeared relaxed and determined. I expressed my desire to work very closely with him. I gave him my home and office telephone numbers and told him that he only had to pick up the telephone and we could talk together on any issue at any time. He gave me his telephone numbers. I assumed we had established from day one that we would work very closely as a team.

I was encouraged to hear from the coal fields that, when he visited the pits and met the miners in the canteen, he was going down well. Scargill's attempts to portray him as an overpaid ogre sent in by Mrs Thatcher to destroy the coal industry were not endorsed by the miners who met him. But not enough met him before the strike started.

That was a great pity, for Ian MacGregor's subsequent inability to communicate was a considerable advantage for Scargill, while those miners who continued to work felt that Ian MacGregor's personality was a disadvantage to them rather than an advantage. They frequently suggested that it would help to defeat Arthur Scargill if Ian MacGregor was quickly replaced.

They were wrong. Nothing would have added more to Scargill's prestige than for it to be seen that he had brought about the downfall of the Chairman of the Coal Board. It would have been particularly wrong because Ian MacGregor was pursuing policies that were correct and sensible. He wanted to put more investment into good pits and the best machinery. He wanted to improve the marketing of coal. He welcomed the Government's generosity in financing early retirement and voluntary redundancy programmes. The government and Ian MacGregor were at one.

The previous Chairman, Sir Norman Siddall, had made considerable progress in eradicating the uneconomic pits. During his period as Chairman many pits had been closed. But the scope for improved productivity remained considerable.

In 1975, the Labour Government had agreed with the Coal Board and the mining unions a Plan for Coal. This envisaged a substantial investment programme in new equipment and machinery and the developing of the better seams. The programme also envisaged that, in return for this, there would be a substantial improvement in productivity.

Over ten years something like £6 billion would be invested in the industry and productivity would increase by 4% a year, said the plan. The targets for investment were fully met. Indeed, when the Conservatives came to power in 1979 the investment programme was increased. Throughout the period of Tory government investment in coal had been higher than envisaged under Labour's Plan for Coal.

But productivity did not respond. Instead of 4% per annum for ten years productivity rose by just 4% over the *whole* decade. The uneconomic pits were the main cause of the bad performance. It took no genius to see that there would be a very substantial improvement in the performance, and therefore the prospects, of the coal industry if they were closed and investment concentrated on the better pits.

I was confident at the prospect we had of transforming the industry without a strike, for I felt that if the facts were successfully communicated to the miners then there would be no way in which Scargill could obtain a successful ballot.

How could there be an industrial dispute when one considered what the Government had decided to inject into this industry:

1 There would not be a single *compulsory* redundancy
2 There would be early retirement provisions for miners over the age of 50 threatened by a pit closure that were more generous than any early retirement provisions offered in any other industry
3 For younger miners, or indeed older miners, there would always be a job available at another pit
4 For younger miners who did not want to transfer to another pit there would be redundancy payments for the voluntary redundancy on better terms than had ever been provided in any industry
5 The Government would commit itself to a capital investment programme of £800 million per year into this industry, a capital investment programme that would make many other industries both nationalized and privately owned exceedingly jealous
6 A pay deal that in spite of the low productivity of the industry would allow the Coal Board to give far more financial benefit to those who produced more

In my discussions with Ian MacGregor we agreed that the right framework for the future investment and closure programmes to be discussed, would be on a regional basis and that in each of the regions the NUM should be fully consulted as to the targets that had to be achieved and the closures that would be involved.

In each region the National Coal Board would be able to make clear that there would be no compulsory redundancies, and inform the miners of the generous early retirement provisions. The National Coal Board would also be able to spell out the large investment programme of more than £2 million a day.

Regions would obviously differ, for some would be more adversely affected by closures than others. Discussions began in early March 1984. It was at the Cortonwood pit that the first moves to go for industrial action without a ballot took place. The matter was clumsily mishandled by management, who were provoked by the NUM refusing to collaborate in the normal way in discussions on a closure.

One manager made a comment, out of his frustration with

the NUM, which could have been taken as meaning that he was going to close Cortonwood without going through the normal agreed procedures with the union.

This was not the case. But it was used as a pretext to start industrial action.

What was disastrous was the failure of management quickly to communicate the facts to each of the individual miners concerned.

I was shocked that the management did not realize that each individual had to be told the facts and that we could not rely upon the NUM leadership to convey the truth. I endeavoured to persuade the Coal Board to send a direct mail letter to each miner confirming categorically that the normal procedures for closure would be followed at Cortonwood, as elsewhere. Incredibly, they did not have the managerial means, or even the names and addresses, to communicate instantly. I then suggested that local press advertising should be used. But by the time they got round to doing anything the situation had deteriorated. On March 4 the Yorkshire NUM called for an indefinite strike.

The Coal Industry National Consultative Meeting took place on March 6 in Scotland, where the cut in output was put to the union by the National Coal Board.

Immediately the Scottish NUM called for an area strike. It was two days after this that Scargill moved to see if he could achieve a national strike without a ballot.

The NUM National Executive meeting on March 8 sanctioned strikes to be conducted on an area by area basis. It refused to hold a ballot throughout the country. For the first time in the history of the union its leader endeavoured, with a few comrades, to get people out on strike without a democratic ballot.

Scargill knew that if the men had time to learn the facts, then there would be no possible question of him succeeding in a ballot for strike action.

March 12 was the first day of the strike and immediately Scargill saw to it that the Yorkshire NUM Executive Committee voted to send pickets to other areas. On March 13 we saw the paid mob mobilized to intimidate other miners throughout the country to join in the industrial action.

There were miners who refused to strike without a ballot and thus one-third of Britain's coal production continued throughout the dispute. Those who did vote, region by region, rejected industrial action by more than two votes to one. Scargill's refusal to ballot was proof that the Government was right in its judgement that there was no good reason for the strike – and that a majority of miners knew it.

Nine areas decided to have a ballot, as did the mechanics and enginemen in Durham. The only vote in favour of a strike was in Northumberland and even there the vote for a strike fell far short of the vote required under union rules for industrial action to be taken. These figures showed clearly that there never was a chance of Scargill winning a ballot.

Area	% *For a Strike*	% *Against a Strike*
Cumberland	22.2	77.8
Derbyshire	49.9	50.1
Leicestershire	10.7	89.3
Midlands	27.1	72.9
Northumberland	52	48
North Wales	31.7	68.3
Nottingham	26.5	73.5
North Western	40.8	59.2
South Derbyshire	16.4	83.6
Durham Mechanics	36	64
Durham Enginemen	14.9	85.1

The dispute had to be conducted recognizing that we were dealing with a ruthless enemy. I decided I would personally take charge of the overall operations and do so by having a group that would meet daily, a group over which I could preside and within which the major government departments and the Coal Board would be fully represented. Each morning, at nine a.m. a meeting would take place in my room at the Energy Department.

The Whitehall machinery responded magnificently to the challenge so I was surprised when Ian MacGregor, of all people, wrote a range of remarks hostile to the Civil Servants both in my Department and throughout Whitehall. It is always easy to hit at bureaucrats because they are unable to reply. But, Ian MacGregor's impression of the skill of the Civil Servants in my Department was best expressed when he came to me one day and asked if I could persuade my retiring Permanent Secretary, Sir Kenneth Couzens, to become the Deputy Chairman of the Coal Board. The request was not expected, but I was delighted because I knew that Sir Kenneth's qualities would mean an enormous injection of ability into the Coal Board. I persuaded him to take the post, not the easiest of tasks had it not been for his sense of public duty.

Every morning a pit-by-pit survey was made. Each day by 9 a.m. we knew the number of men who were working at each pit in each district. We had a summary of incidents and acts of violence. We were able to hear of the adverse and sometimes favourable effects upon firms throughout the country. From the beginning it was easy to see that the pickets were to be the front line troops of the Scargill campaign.

The first targets were the pits that had voted to continue to work. Coach and car loads of paid pickets descended upon these pits and, using methods of intimidation and violence, endeavoured to close the working pits. They failed in this task partly due to the determination of the miners who had balloted to continue to work and partly because of the courage and bravery of the individual policemen. 1399 policemen were injured during the dispute. Without their sacrifices and without their injuries Scargill would have succeeded and it would have meant that Britain was a place where the mob and not the rule of law prevailed.

There were other moments when the media, some industrialists and some Tory MPs considered that the easy way to end the picketing was to use legislation recently passed by taking the NUM to the courts for illegal picketing.

When there was clear evidence that the Yorkshire NUM had organized mass picketing at locations outside their own responsibilities an injunction was sought and obtained. The Yorkshire NUM then transferred the responsibilities for picketing to the NUM Executive. To have followed up the injunction against the Yorkshire NUM would not have succeeded, for they were no longer organizing such picketing. The Coal Board could have brought an injunction against the NUM Executive but when they succeeded they would find that the future picketing was organized by some other organization or group and when they obtained an injunction against them another group would take over the organization.

Nothing would have delighted Arthur Scargill more than a series of injunctions in the courts that in practice failed to stop the mass picketing taking place.

When he failed to close the Nottingham pits he decided an easier target was the steelworkers where there were fewer locations, and where the input of raw materials was not just of coal but of iron ore. Again the police succeeded in seeing that all legal traffic going to the steelworks succeeded in getting through. The steelworkers themselves had no desire to destroy their prospects by supporting a man who refused to ballot his own members. The steelworkers not only continued to produce but improved their productivity.

The railways ran too, despite the desire of their leaders to support Scargill. For me perhaps the best moment in the dispute was when one Sunday evening I was telephoned by a signalman who explained to me he was at a signal box in a mining area which was still at work and that the signalman on the other shift was a communist who stopped every coal train coming through. 'I will phone you each Sunday evening and tell you when I am on shift for the coming week and you send all the coal trains through then.'

The lorry driver, the train driver and the power worker all decided that a trade union leader who refused to ballot his own members and who was clearly out to topple the government of the day was not a man who deserved their enthusiastic support. They were right, because the Government was not out to destroy the coal industry, but to see it survive.

Scargill's objective during the strike was to secure agreement that no pit should be closed until it was totally exhausted – a demand which no management of any coal industry anywhere in the world had ever or could ever fulfill. It was then I knew that his motivation was essentially political.

Early on I took a different view from the Chairman of the Coal Board as to the potential length of the strike. Ian MacGregor treated the strike as a conventional industrial affair.

He considered it was developing in an identical way to the strike that had taken place in the steel industry. I pointed out that Bill Sirs was no Marxist, but a decent Trade Unionist who took industrial action out of desperation in the hope of lowering the redundancies that were necessary. But Scargill was a politically motivated man who looked upon this as a major political offensive. Mr MacGregor said that he thought the duration of the strike was likely to be a similar period to that of the steel dispute, as after this period the men could see that there was no point in continuing and they would wish to go back.

But the men were likely to be kept out on this occasion by violence and by force. No such violence and force had ever been needed in the steel dispute because the men had balloted for industrial action and totally supported the action taking place. None of them bothered to cross picket lines. I advised the Government that this could well be a very long dispute.

I took the action that was necessary to see that the stocks at our power stations were preserved and that the maximum oil burn (the use of oil-fired power stations which under normal circumstances lie dormant) took place immediately. The speed with which the switch to oil burn took place, the speed with which the maximum coal was continued to be distributed to the power stations, the speed with which we were able to organize the pattern of distribution, learning from the mistakes we had made in 1974, was a very impressive operation and vital to our success.

But Scargill continually deceived the miners about the state of coal stocks. On 6th February he told them that there were only eight weeks of stocks at the power stations. After the dispute started on television on 29th March he said there were only nine to ten weeks of stocks at the power stations. In the *Morning Star* of 30th March he said there were two months stocks at the power stations. On 21st April he publicly declared there were eight to nine weeks. At a rally in Mansfield on 7th May he said eight weeks. At the National Union of Railwaymen's Conference on 26th June he said there would be cuts in the power stations in August.

The reality was that we were never anywhere near to the stocks running out. The figures that the miners were given were untrue; they were figures intended to make them feel there were only a few more weeks to go, when in fact there was no prospect of power cuts taking place.

I pleaded with Ian MacGregor to improve the communications of the Coal Board. They had made a good offer to the miners. They genuinely wanted the industry to succeed. They had a good case to communicate. But Ian MacGregor was not good at doing this himself. When confronted with an opposing point of view, he tends to be silent rather than being speedy in reply. On many occasions he appeared as a man tired and under pressure. He *was* tired and under pressure.

It is extraordinary looking back that it took three months before I could persuade the Coal Board to send a letter to individual miners explaining the true background to the dispute. It was Monday, 18th June 1984 before such a letter went. I was able to play a part in the drafting of this letter in order to make it totally clear that the Scargill charges about butchering the industry were completely unfounded, that the investment was high, and that no compulsory redundancies would take place. It would certainly have been to the advantage of all concerned if such a letter had been despatched at a much earlier date.

The letter read as follows:

Dear Colleague,

Your future in danger

I am taking the unusual step of writing to you at home because I want every man and woman who has a stake in the coal industry to realize clearly the damage which will be done if this disastrous strike goes on a long time.

The leaders of the NUM have talked of it continuing into the winter. Now that our talks with them have broken down this is a real possibility. It could go on until December or even longer. In which case the consequences for everybody will be very grave.

Your President talks continually of keeping the strike going indefinitely until he achieves 'victory'.

I would like to tell you, not provocatively or as a threat, why that will not happen however long the strike lasts.

What the strike is really about is that the NUM leadership is denying our right to manage the coal industry in the way we think is most efficient, best, and in the interests of those who work in it. We want to build a high-volume, highly paid, low-cost industry which will be profitable and competitive with foreign coal producers. That is why we are spending up to £800 million per year on your industry.

Our plan means, in the short term, cutting out some uneconomic pits and making about 20 000 men redundant by voluntary methods and with very generous redundancy if they do not wish to take alternative jobs in the industry. It also means a more secure future for those who remain.

I want it to be known that however long the strike goes on we shall not hand over management and decision making to your President and his colleagues.

But the second reason why continuing the strike will not bring the NUM 'victory' is this: in the end nobody will win. Everybody will lose – and lose disastrously.

Many of you have already lost more than £2000 in earnings and have seen your savings disappear. If the strike goes on until December it will take many of you years to recover financially and also more jobs may be lost – and all for nothing.

Your President has accused us of planning to butcher the industry. I have no such intention or desire. I want to build up the industry into one we can all be proud to be part of.

But if we cannot return to reality and get back to work then the industry may well be butchered. But the butchers will not be the Coal Board.

You are all aware that mines which are not constantly maintained and worked deteriorate in terms of safety and workability.

At the present time there are between 20 and 30 pits which are viable which will be in danger of never re-opening if we have a lengthy strike.

This is a strike which should never have happened. It is based on very serious misrepresentation and distortion of the facts. At great financial cost miners have supported the strike for fourteen weeks because your leaders have told you this:

That the Coal Board is out to butcher the coal industry
That we plan to do away with 70 000 jobs
That we plan to close down about 86 pits, leaving only 100 working collieries.

If these things were true I would not blame miners for getting angry or for being deeply worried. *But these things are absolutely untrue.* I state that categorically and solemnly. You have been deliberately misled.

Only the NUM which called the strike, can end it.

I would like you to consider carefully, away from the violence and pressures of the mass pickets, whether this strike is in your interests. I ask you to join your associates who already have returned to work so that we can start repairing the damage and building up a good future.

Yours sincerely,
Ian MacGregor

I urged Ian MacGregor to find a person to communicate on TV. Eventually he told me he had found a man from Yorkshire called Michael Eaton. When I met Michael Eaton I was impressed by a man who loved the industry. He was a warm Yorkshireman with a desire to see that the industry was not destroyed by a Marxist.

When Michael Eaton communicated well on radio and television, he had to withstand many pressures from within the Coal Board of men jealous of his high profile. I was shocked when, after his appointment, a major negotiation took place between the Coal Board and the NUM he was banned from the office and not allowed to be present. I expressed my surprise and concern that a man appointed to communicate was not going to be present at a very crucial and important meeting where the whole of the media would be waiting outside for comments from the Coal Board's spokesman. Ian MacGregor told me that, because of the publicity that Michael Eaton had obtained, he was creating jealousies within the Coal Board and that some top men had threatened to resign if Michael Eaton was allowed to go to the meeting. Those people had succeeded in making Ian MacGregor prevent the man he had appointed to communicate from communicating.

After months of effort, Scargill had failed to close a single pit or a single steel works. Throughout the coal fields there was recognition that Scargill's methods were not succeeding. Scargill saw the need for a success after so many failures. He chose as the location for his major effort the small plant at Orgreave.

Orgreave is a small coke works with difficult access in the heart of the area where Scargill had mobilized the most militant support. He warned the media to watch Orgreave.

He mobilized thousands of pickets. He personally led the action and on the 30th May was arrested at Orgreave.

Every day thousands of pickets were mobilized at Orgreave. Every day for eight consecutive days. The police suffered considerable injuries and casualties. But every load of coke went from Orgreave to its location. The attempt by Scargill to have one victory by the method of the mob had failed, and if I was asked what perhaps was the great turning point in this dispute it was this proof that the mob would never succeed.

But the militant left still felt that they could succeed. The coal industry was debated in the House of Commons and Mr Benn, one of Scargill's active supporters expressed his total confidence that the Government would be defeated.

There was clear evidence that the militant left and Mr Scargill did not have the support of sensible trade unionists. The TUC carried out days of action. The NUR called for one-day strikes in support of the miners. The other railway union urged its members to stop moving coal. The Transport and General Workers' Union expressed their sympathy but the result was the railwaymen continued to move the coal, the lorry drivers continued to move the coal.

At the beginning of July the TUC decided not to accept the NUM's request for a halt to steel production. What a total act of folly it would have been to have destroyed the steel industry in order to support someone who was doing his best to destroy the coal industry.

There was the same determination of ordinary trade unionists not to undermine their own jobs when the threatened dock strike of July 1984 swiftly came to an end.

Throughout the summer our success at moving coal to the power stations was remarkable. We did it by lorry, by train, and we massively increased the oil burn at the power stations, much of both oil and coal coming by ship. The nuclear power stations were performing well, industry was being prudent in its use of energy without diminishing its production.

I knew that if by the methods he was using Arthur Scargill was able to prolong the strike there remained the potential of greater coal imports and the movement of coal stocks from striking mines. I knew that we would succeed.

I told the Prime Minister that we had endurance for at least another year, and later I was able to tell her that we had endurance for at least two years.

The mining MPs in the House on both sides increasingly recognized that the strike was doomed to failure.

In September, when the new Bishop of Durham was enthroned at Durham Cathedral, he decided to use the event to attack both the Government and the National Coal Board. Few people knew of the political beliefs of the bishop and perhaps felt that his was the genuine Christian approach to the dispute. Television, radio and the press gave considerable publicity to this viewpoint. Decent people would be deeply concerned that a Bishop in a mining area condemned the Board and the Government and had little criticism of Scargill and the organized mobs.

I was deeply concerned because there had never been any moment when I felt that the actions that were being pursued and the offers that were being made were anything other than Christian. Obviously as far as my prayers were concerned and my attempt to apply Christianity into the practical realms of politics I had endeavoured to see that the approach to the miners was decent and compassionate and was understanding of their personal and social problems.

I set out my views in a correspondence that I attach as an appendix to this essay. I think it was right to distinguish between the Bishop's political views, which are considerable and sincerely held, and the suggestion that his particular view of politics is part of the Christian ethic.

Arthur Scargill was boosted by the Labour Party conference of 1984. It was a conference with a new leader, Neil Kinnock, dominated by a Marxist trade union leader striking without a ballot, Arthur Scargill. The ovations, the cheers, the enthusiasm was all for him. Neil Kinnock made a pathetic performance and failed to stand up to Scargill. When Neil Kinnock is defeated at the next General Election he may reflect on his failure to do the right things during the coal dispute.

When Scargill went to him as leader of the Labour party and said he wished to change the rules on voting so that instead of a two-thirds majority he should only have to have 51% Mr Kinnock agreed to support him. All Mr Kinnock had to say was 'yes, providing you immediately go for a ballot.' Kinnock just said 'yes' and never did demand a ballot.

The second opportunity was when Kinnock knew that violence was taking place by paid mobs of pickets. He could easily have said he supported the miners in their dispute but insisted that the NUM complied with the TUC guidelines on picketing and that only six pickets operating without violence would be at any gate. Arthur Scargill would have found it difficult to continue the mob picketing. Kinnock would have been praised and thanked by the nation for bringing an end to this horrific spectacle. But, alas, the Labour leader failed to utter a word of criticism of Mr Scargill's methods.

The electorate observed a Labour party leader who was pleasant on television but weak in political courage. If Kinnock had stood up to Scargill during the dispute it would have been good for the Labour party and bad for the Tory party – which, as a Tory, I could argue was bad for the nation. But if you are confronted with the extraordinary threat that Arthur Scargill represented it is a time for all democrats in the nation to be united in their purpose.

Eighteen months after the dispute had ended the impact of Scargill upon Kinnock remained. At the 1986 Labour Party Conference the Labour party passed a motion acceptable to Scargill which would phase out Britain's nuclear industry. It was a motion which if put into operation would mean that at the very time that North Sea oil and gas was disappearing a Labour Government would eradicate the availability of nuclear energy. Scargill's ambition would be fulfilled, the British economy totally dependent upon himself. The Labour party leaders who have previously held office must have known how disastrous such an agreement would be. But under the pressure of Scargill that became official Labour party policy.

I became concerned at reports I was receiving from the various mining areas that NACODS, the union whose members were the middle management of the mines, and the men responsible for safety in them, were concerned that their members were being wrongly treated.

In my meeting with Conservative Members of Parliament representing coal-mining constituencies, I found growing anxiety that the members of NACODS were becoming very hostile to the way that they were being treated by the Coal Board Management.

I discussed this at our regular meetings with Mr MacGregor and stressed the importance that Mr Scargill obtained no satisfaction from another union in the coal industry being discontented and dissatisfied. Mr MacGregor was very confident that no such problem existed. He said that there were one or two collieries where personalities were causing a problem but nothing serious.

At a further meeting with Ian MacGregor I pointed out that these were the men upon whom we were dependent to see that the working pits continued working and the striking pits were retained in a position of safety, so that the miners would have pits to return to.

Ian MacGregor again argued that there were individual problems affecting personalities and gave his own assessment that the leaders of NACODS were making a good deal of noise, but that they were a union with a long tradition of not taking industrial action and he felt this was a tradition that would continue.

On 12 September the warnings I had given proved to be justified when the NACODS Executive voted to ballot their members recommending a strike on three issues: the Board's cut back in capacity; its attitudes to conciliation procedures; and the issue that directly affected them – the guidelines requiring NACODS members to make attempts to cross picket lines before qualifying for pay.

Ian MacGregor said that the ballot paper was exceedingly

vague and that by putting all three issues, it meant that NACODS members were not going to vote on only one issue. The NACODS leaders were posturing in order to try and get a strong negotiating position with the Coal Board, he said, adding that they were not a union which would lose their pay and salaries by industrial action.

I urged that the Coal Board mount a vigorous campaign to convey to NACODS members that the Board would wish to operate sensible guidelines for NACODS members in striking areas; would wish to rationalize the industry to make it a better industry; and would continue to see that there would be no compulsory redundancies and that all NUM members would be treated in a generous and civilized way.

I wanted the National Coal Board to do a direct mail campaign to all NACODS members. I was assured that the management would be doing all in their power to communicate. In reality very little effective communicating took place. Those advocating a strike did all the talking. Those recognizing the dangers of such a strike were quiet.

The effects of NACODS going on strike were potentially an enormous boost to Mr Scargill at a very crucial time. This support should not have emerged. With proper management it never would have emerged. A NACODS strike would close down the working pits for the NACODS members were essential for safety, without them production would have to cease.

The result of the ballot was on 28 September: 82.5% of NACODS voted in favour of strike action. At this moment Mr MacGregor's tone changed. He too expressed anxiety. He discussed whether it would not be possible for legislation to be introduced so that outside experts and contractors could take over the safety requirements so that the working pits could continue to work. He did *not* at that time express the view that if a strike did take place the Nottinghamshire NACODS members would continue to work.

Knowing the tradition of the trade unions after a genuinely democratic ballot I believed that it would be very unlikely that they would continue to work. The NACODS ballot was a great boost to Mr Scargill's morale at that time and hurt the return to work. It was vital that the NACODS disagreements be settled. I emphasized this to Mr MacGregor and suggested to him ways that did not undermine the authority of the management of the Coal Board.

Following their ballot I received a request for a meeting from the NACODS executive. In all my years as a minister I have made it my invariable practice to agree to see any trade union leader connected with my Department. As the son of a shop steward, I have always recognized the importance of the trade union movement, and I have always been in favour of a good dialogue with trade unionists.

When I received the NACODS request therefore, I naturally told the NCB of the request and proceeded to arrange the meeting. At this and later meetings I listened to the anxieties and viewpoint of the NACODS representatives, and reported them to the NCB. Throughout these exchanges it was clear between the NACODS representatives, the NCB, and myself that while I was happy to meet the NACODS delegation, I was not prepared to negotiate with them on the substance of the dispute – that was the job of the NCB. My task was simply to ensure that their views were understood both by the NCB and my colleagues in the government.

Despite the meeting both refused to accept the proposals that ACAS put forward and on the 16 October the NACODS National Executive gave notice of strike action to start at 6 a.m. on 25 October.

Then agreement was reached between the NCB and NACODS on 23 October and NACODS called the strike off unconditionally the following day. The agreement they reached was reasonable. It gave clear guidance as to the manner in which NACODS officials would be treated in those areas in which the strike was taking place.

The 1984 TUC Congress had instructed the TUC Inner Cabinet to attempt to mediate in the miner's strike. When, therefore, some weeks later, I received a request to meet a TUC delegation I immediately agreed – applying the same rule as I had applied to the request from NACODS.

An impressive array of the most famous people in the trade union movement came to my Department to discuss the dispute. I told them of my genuine hopes for the industry, of the generosity of the proposals we were making, of the lack of any reason for an industrial dispute, and of the interests of the nation and the trade union movement that such a dispute should be ended. I pointed out to them that if any of them had obtained by negotiation a pay offer, the guarantee against a single compulsory redundancy and the early retirement provisions that we had offered to the miners they would be boasting of their achievements and not deploring the offer that they had obtained.

It was the first time I had met Norman Willis, the new TUC General Secretary. I had known his predecessors, and respected them. I respected Norman Willis. The meeting produced no solution but the press were handled in such a way by both the TUC and the Government that it produced no deterioration.

Those unions that had been present at the meeting could not have felt that there was any case for active support of Mr Scargill. With no effective support from other unions with more economic clout than the NUM possessed there was no chance of Mr Scargill succeeding.

The responsible members of the TUC had recognized that this was not a Tory Government acting in an irresponsible way towards the miners. Many of them also knew the damage it was doing to other trade unionists who were adversely affected by the dispute and the damage it was doing to the reputation of the TUC.

Money coming in from the Soviet Union: secret trips to Libya; these were not the types of ingredient that the more responsible British trade unionists wished to be part of the trade union scene.

Throughout the dispute there was never a meeting with trade unionists or indeed a conversation with trade unionists that the Coal Board were not told about, and always after such conversations or meetings had taken place the Coal Board were fully briefed. As to the meeting with the TUC itself, discussions did take place with Mr MacGregor. It was agreed with Mr MacGregor that the damage done by a refusal of a Cabinet Minister to meet or talk with the TUC would be very considerable and could well have mobilized other trade unions in support of Mr Scargill.

It was agreed with Mr MacGregor that I would make it very clear to the TUC that any negotiations upon a settlement could only take place between the Coal Board and the NUM. The meeting with the TUC had taken place in December. After the Christmas break the return to work continued and accelerated as more and more miners realized there was no justification for the industrial action and that their leadership had not only deprived them of a vote but had taken the wrong decision.

The trade union movement knew I had no desire to humiliate or embarrass the miners; I genuinely admired the miners and was deeply depressed at the hardship that many of them and their families were suffering.

On 21 January 1985, with the return to work increasing daily, Mr Peter Heathfield and Mr Mick McGahy of the NUM met Ned Smith of the NCB for talks on the possibility of resuming negotiations.

Mr Scargill made it clear that he would offer talks without preconditions but it was naturally known that the only reason Mr Scargill wanted talks without preconditions was that, whilst talks were taking place, the return to work would almost certainly end.

It was vital to ascertain that the NUM were genuinely willing to address themselves to the basic issue: that they must remove the absurdity of their demand that every pit, no matter how uneconomic, should remain open until it was exhausted of coal.

At the beginning of February, talks took place between Peter Heathfield and Ned Smith and attempts were made to see if some negotiations could take place. The Coal Board made it clear that no talks could take place unless they dealt with the question of uneconomic capacity. At the same time as the discussions between Peter Heathfield and Ned Smith, the TUC initiated another round of negotiations which played an important role in bringing the dispute to an end. Several conflicting versions of these discussions have emerged. Since the result of the discussions was to pave the way for the defeat of the Scargillite tendency, and the victory of common sense, I regard it as important to set the record straight as to what actually happened.

Following the approach by the TUC, Mr MacGregor and Mr Willis arranged to meet to try to agree to terms to settle the dispute which the TUC would be willing to recommend to the NUM. Mr MacGregor decided to take to that meeting a draft document that he had prepared. Mr MacGregor promised me that the draft would be submitted to me before the meeting. No such draft arrived. My office contacted his office and I was informed that the document was on the way to my office. The document arrived at five minutes to four and the meeting was to start at four o'clock.

I was shocked when I examined the document. Had it been handed to the TUC, it would have given them a document capable of interpretation by Mr Scargill as a victory.

I immediately telephoned Mr MacGregor. I told him that if he handed this document over, the Government would have to express clearly the fact that it considered it a wholly unsatisfactory document.

The draft that Ian MacGregor prepared was not handed to Mr Willis, who was told instead that a draft would be forthcoming.

The draft made references which would have enabled Mr Scargill to interpret the words to mean that the Coal Board would have an obligation to see that pit closures did not take place during a period of high unemployment.

There were loose words and phrases such as 'deemed exhausted' which did not make clear whether deeming would have to be with the approval of both sides or just in the view of the Coal Board.

It was an agreement which would have enabled Mr Scargill

to say he had reached a settlement whilst retaining the freedom of the NUM to continue its policy of opposing the closure of pits for economic reasons.

It was a document that made mention of a new independent body in a manner that pit closures could have been totally delayed as long as the NUM failed to reach agreement upon the detail of that independent body.

The document that was subsequently presented to the TUC was a draft that had total clarity and would not enable one side to interpret words in a completely different way from the other side.

A fudged settlement would have been disastrous. It would have meant that the many sacrifices that had been made to see that sanity and democracy prevailed would have been made in vain.

The TUC did receive from Mr MacGregor a clear document which was acceptable to the Government. They asked if they could see the Prime Minister and then come to my office as a delegation to discuss this document and make sure that it would have the backing of the Government. I discussed the necessity of doing this with Mr MacGregor and he agreed that such a meeting had to take place.

I arranged to lunch with Ian MacGregor after the TUC meeting with the Prime Minister so that I could brief him and agree to the details of the negotiations.

The lunch that took place at La Capannina was a foursome, Ian MacGregor being accompanied by Tim Bell and I was accompanied by David Hunt. Following the meeting that had taken place with the TUC at 10 Downing Street I was confident that the TUC were taking a responsible view of the situation and we discussed at the lunch the two minor drafting changes that were needed and Ian MacGregor readily accepted these.

I suggested to Ian MacGregor that Tim Bell could, if he wished, be at my office that evening before the TUC arrived and remain in another office whilst they were there so that if I needed to consult with Ian MacGregor he would have a personal lieutenant there who could contact him and discuss things. Ian MacGregor agreed to this course of action. To my horror when Tim Bell arrived at the office he informed me that he was depressed that Ian MacGregor had changed his mind during the course of the afternoon. He said this was because another adviser had suggested to Ian MacGregor that the only reason I was trying to reach an agreement was to achieve a settlement during the Prime Minister's absence in Washington. She was flying to Washington that evening.

The other adviser suggested to Ian MacGregor that if he stuck to his original wording without any change any settlement could be delayed until after the Prime Minister returned. It was fortunate that this absurd point had been made whilst there was still time to do something about it.

I contacted 10 Downing Street and they delivered to Ian MacGregor the clear message that the Prime Minister wanted the document as agreed to be the basis of our discussions with the TUC.

The TUC meeting went well. Tim Bell congratulated me on the final version of the document. I agreed with Tim Bell that we would meet early the next morning with Ian MacGregor to agree the final version of the document and also the version of the covering letter that should go with it.

The meeting took place the next morning. It was cordial and in total agreement.

I was shocked when that afternoon my Press Officer informed me that four journalists had contacted her office with the story that the previous evening, whilst meeting the TUC, I had wanted to make a long list of concessions but that Ian MacGregor had refused to agree to this. One of the four journalists said he had received this brief from Mr MacGregor's advisers. I therefore asked my Press Officer, Romilla Christopherson, to come into my office where I was having a meeting with Ian MacGregor. I confronted Ian MacGregor with this incredible story and I asked him to confirm to my Press Officer that this story was totally untrue so that she could then inform the four journalists that Ian MacGregor had personally made it clear to her that there was no truth in this story. This Ian MacGregor did and the Press Officer was able to tell the press that he had personally denied to her any validity in the story.

Had the journalists not contacted her office, had Ian MacGregor not been in my office at the time, had I not been able to ask him to deny the story in front of my Press Officer, there is no doubt that the next day four newspapers would have carried the story that Peter Walker had wished to make concessions to the TUC and had been stopped by the intervention of Ian MacGregor.

Ian MacGregor expressed his total agreement with the document and the covering letter. I warned him of the further concessions the TUC would undoubtedly press for and I told him it was vital that none of these concessions were given. He agreed.

He later reported that the TUC had pressed him to give way on the points I had mentioned to him that morning. He confirmed that he told them it was impossible as the document was now in its final form and he expressed the view that they would endeavour to persuade the NUM to accept this document.

The negotiations with the TUC did not extend the strike. Quite the contrary. The manner in which Mr Scargill immediately rejected the TUC document convinced the TUC that they were dealing with a person who had a deep desire to continue with industrial action for political purposes and had no desire to come to a reasonable and sensible settlement. It was after Mr Scargill's rejection of the TUC document that the return to work accelerated, for it was clear that no other union in the country would give him any support. It was clear that the strike was very near to its end.

The moderates in the Labour party recognized only too well the damage that Arthur Scargill was doing to their party and the urgency of trying to bring an end to the dispute. It was clear in the statements I was able to make that the coal stocks after the Christmas break were on a scale that there was no danger to the power supplies of Britain for more than a year to come. The increasing return to work showed quite clearly there was no possibility of this political action succeeding. The NUM Executive throughout had been under great personal pressure from Arthur Scargill and decided that the only course was to go for a return to work without there being any agreement or settlement. So ended the tragedy of this dispute.

There are lessons to be learnt from the manner in which the Government attempted to tackle the serious social and economic problems of rationalizing the coal industry. There may well be other industries where one has to introduce generous early retirement provisions to ease the process of rationalization. For miners to retire in their mid-fifties on a generous pension is no bad thing. The nature of their work makes early retirement a reasonable reward for the work they have done.

In other industries a similar approach to early retirement would make a contribution to reducing unemployment in this country and replacing some of those who are currently unemployed with people who are happily retired.

There is the important lesson of the Enterprise Company that was created to try to bring new jobs into those mining areas where the collieries were being closed. I was pleased to read in Mr MacGregor's book that he considered this was a good idea. I had several meetings to persuade him to pursue such a course. He first of all informed me that he considered that the steel industry had wasted money in this way. He then informed me that anything he wished to do could in any case be carried out within the Coal Board itself and he needed no special company in order to do it. Under continuous pressure from me he agreed to create the new Enterprise Company. It did then get under way. It has now been a remarkable success.

I started off by offering the Enterprise Company enough money to get it under way and stating that as soon as it had used the money effectively more would be available. I then doubled the amount of money and then doubled it again and now have provided £40 million to that Company to carry out schemes, concepts and ideas to bring new jobs to the mining areas. The first £20 million it spent on new enterprises, and existing enterprises in mining areas attracted a further £100 million of outside investment. So £20 million of Government money in fact created £120 million of investment in new jobs in coal mining areas. The total number of jobs provided was 12 500 and on this parallel it means when the existing £40 million has been utilized 25 000 new jobs will have been created in coal mining areas where pits have closed.

This is a figure equivalent to the voluntary redundancies that have taken place as a result of the rationalization of 1985/86. These will be jobs unlike the ones which they replace, they will not be jobs in pits fast approaching exhaustion but jobs in new businesses, many of them with great scope for further expansion. They will give to the children of the miners a diversity of job opportunities which in many mining communities has never been available.

It would be quite wrong to imagine that the success of the enterprise company lies only in its ability to provide public funds. The fact that it has been able to attract substantial private finances into it as well is of course important. But another important element has been its ability to use redundant property. Many colliery workshops and other surface buildings have been converted into low cost workshops which have allowed small businesses to get started with minimum overheads. The company's work has also provided management support from within British Coal. NCB enterprises has therefore worked by bringing together public and private resources, financial material and personnel. It is an outstanding example of the success which results from practical co-operation between public and private sectors.

I believe we must learn from the lessons of the 'multiplier effect' of such companies and I hope when other major industries, whether in the private or public sector, have to face important rationalization with the potential unemployment it could bring will examine ways in which this sort of application of finance and existing skills and existing buildings can be converted into new jobs and new commercial activity to the benefit of the families and the communities that are involved.

The tragedy of this dispute is emphasised by comparing what happened with what should have happened. The NUM, under inspired leadership, eager to improve the lot of the miners, could have negotiated with the Coal Board the most marvellous package to the benefit of the industry and those who worked in it.

There was available agreement on substantial capital investment in the years ahead. There was available a productivity deal under which the miner would have received his share of the improved productivity that would come from the new capital investment and a removal of restrictive practices and inefficient working by the men. There was available an agreement whereby no one would be made compulsorily redundant and the availability of early retirement would have provided a quality of conditions for the industry never enjoyed by almost any other industry.

Never on any occasion did Mr Scargill endeavour to negotiate such possibilities. He adhered to the one simplistic slogan that no pit no matter how uneconomic should ever be closed. Events since the coal dispute ended have illustrated the potential that existed. Productivity in the industry has improved from 2.4 tons per man shift prior to the dispute to an average of 3.6 per shift after the dispute, an increase of 50%.

It is sad for the industry that having improved its performance a lower oil price brings in a form of competition which it is difficult to meet. But that was always a danger to the coal industry and a danger that it can resist far more successfully with high standards of efficiency than with the previous uneconomic performance.

Britain still possesses some of the largest coal reserves in western Europe. We have a mining machinery industry as good as any in the world. We have the potential for a successful coal mining industry for decades to come. But it will only be achieved if the industry ceases to be the centre of activity for Marxist politicians and becomes an industry with a real sense of participation by all involved. A working colliery is very much a team effort and the coal industry is an industry to which the concept of employee cooperatives could apply well. Unfortunately, instead of embracing such a concept, the industry is weighed down by the centralised bureaucracy imposed on it when it was nationalised. If the confidence of the industry is restored and new standards of productivity are reached careful thought should be given as to the way in which that industry could be given the freedom in which the miner would have a real sense of participation and a direct reward for the success that was achieved.

There are further fundamental lessons to be learnt from the coal dispute.

1 The nation must never allow the paid and organized mob to prevail. If any such threat exists those responsible for upholdinging law and order must be in a position to resist it
2 All firms great and small must see that management communicates the realities to the employee and does not rely on this being done through negotiation with trade union leaders. For far too many years Coal Board management negotiated with the NUM leadership and only too frequently the facts provided by management, the arguments put forward by management, never reached the ears of the individual miner. They heard what the NUM leadership wished them to hear and they had to make their judgements upon that knowledge. Since the dispute much more has been done colliery by colliery to communicate the real facts to the men. That must be a continuing feature in this and every other industry
3 More should be done by governments to give the individual trade unionist the right to a secret ballot, be it a ballot for the leadership of his union at intervals or to decide whether or not to take industrial action. If a ballot had been taken there would never have

been a coal dispute in 1984 and 1985. But the law was such that no such ballot needed to take place

4 Management of industries must acquire the art of being able to communicate to their customers and the public at large. Until the appointment of Michael Eaton the Coal Board failed miserably in this task. They did succeed in distributing coal to their customers and it was a very remarkable tribute to Malcolm Edwards, the man responsible, who did that with such skill. But for many months the British nation was not given the real facts by the management of the issues of the dispute. I was able to do it as a politician but the views of a politician are heavily discounted by those who do not support his political party. The views cogently put across by a good and genuine management have a far wider acceptance

This was a political action and one in which Scargill the leader of that political action could not compromise, for if he had compromised he would have defeated his objective of doing immense damage to a democratically elected Conservative Government.

I was determined to see that the entire parliamentary party was fully briefed throughout the dispute. I did this by a series of personal letters, ten of them in all, in which at various stages of the dispute I wrote to each of our MPs explaining the situation, giving facts and details and enabling them to be fully briefed as far as their constituents were concerned.

Because of the size of our majority there were a very substantial number of coal-mining constituencies where the MP was Conservative. I contacted forty-three Tory Members from coal mining constituencies and arranged for them to come in for personal briefings at frequent intervals. I arranged that they should keep me informed of any developments they discovered and a great deal of the information I received came from Conservative MPs who obtained a good close working relationship with working miners. In non-working areas we had plenty of connections with wives of miners who wished their husbands were not on strike and members of NACODs and other mining unions. The first warning I gave to Ian MacGregor of my concern about the dispute with NACODs came as a result of the number of anxious views that were being expressed to me by Conservative MPs.

The Prime Minister had appointed me to be responsible for the handling of this dispute. There was never a moment throughout the dispute in which I did not have her full and active support. At meetings of ministers I was enabled to inform all of the ministers directly affected by the dispute as to what was occurring and what decisions and actions needed to be taken.

I saw to it that every day the Prime Minister was informed of all of the events that had occurred. There was never any disunity in the Cabinet. I had the full backing of the Prime Minister and there was never a moment when she was not fully aware of what was happening.

The dispute lasted a year, and at times it was very bitter. There was a great deal of injury and violence. There was always anxiety as to damage that could be done to commerce and industry and yet the Cabinet, the Parliamentary Party and the Party in the country remained totally united.

I believe that there is no other political party in Britain that could have retained such loyalty and kept such determination to see that the forces of democracy did prevail.

How different it would have been if a Labour Government had been confronted with the totally unreasonable and outrageous demands of Mr Scargill. Mr Kinnock's performance throughout the dispute was the performance of a man who was under the control and influence of Mr Scargill rather than having any influence on him.

The Alliance again was divided. David Owen did recognize the reality of the Scargill-related industrial action. David Steel did not. He quickly voiced his desire for compromise. He failed to ever give the Government the support that it deserved from any believer in democracy.

I am certain that the unity of a Conservative Cabinet, a

Conservative Parliamentary Party and a Conservative Party in the country was a decisive element in preserving democracy in Britain.

APPENDIX

The exchange of letters between Peter Walker and the Bishop of Durham

Department of Energy,
Millbank,
London SW1

24 September 1984

The Rt Rev. the Lord Bishop of Durham
Auckland Castle
Bishop Auckland
County Durham
DL14 7NR

Dear Bishop,

We have not met but I write because we must share many concerns and many hopes. As a member of the church of which you are a bishop, I certainly share your desire that the spirit of Christianity prevails and with you deplore the existence of poverty, misery, violence and despair.

My personal approach to politics has always reflected a definition of patriotism which desires that every person born a citizen of our country rejoices in that birthright. This therefore demands social and economic policies that eradicate poverty and despair and give all families reasons to rejoice.

You are the Bishop responsible for the diocese of Durham; I am the Minister responsible for energy. We both have responsibility for the miners, their families and their communities.

I was privileged in the early 1970s, when I was the first Secretary of State for the Environment, to have the power to improve the quality of life of the miners in your diocese. I was appalled at the depressing effect on mining communities of living in an environment dominated by slagheaps. I was equally appalled at the poor housing conditions in which many of them had to live – housing conditions devoid of many modern amenities. I launched a campaign which certainly had never previously been surpassed to remove and landscape the slagheaps and to modernize the housing. Hundreds of such schemes have been completed in the mining areas of the North East. A great majority of post-war council housing was modernized, as were many of the homes owned by miners or by the Coal Board. I recall this, not as a personal boast, but because I believe it illustrates the importance of using the resources of a democratically elected government to improve the life of families in the mining communities.

Now I have responsibility again, responsibility which I share with you, to give our miners and their families a future that will bring them and their communities an improved quality of life and greater happiness.

You have preached that the miners must not be 'defeated'. But you have not clarified who is trying to defeat them. You imply that it is Mr MacGregor and the Government. Such an implication has no justification whatsoever.

We have never tried to defeat the miners. We have tried to see that they were victorious to a degree unsurpassed in the history of the mining industry. We tried to give them the guarantee of a better life, devoid of any industrial strike or unrest. Please examine as a Christian bishop the sequence of events which occurred before Mr Scargill decided for the first time in your lifetime to call a national strike in his industry without giving his members the right of a ballot:

1 The Government, without pressure, invested £650 million more in the coal industry than had been agreed under the 'Plan for Coal', which was endorsed by the Labour Government and the National Union of Mineworkers.

2 In spite of the insolvency of the National Coal Board, the Government agreed to provide a further £3000 million to invest in new collieries, better coal faces and better machinery in the years immediately ahead. A policy in sharp contrast to the Government of France, which has decided to halve its coal industry, and in Germany, where the coal industry is also planned to decline substantially.

3 Mr MacGregor, whose departure you request, became the first Chairman of the NCB to declare that every miner who wished to continue working in the industry would be able to do so. In the whole post-war period since nationalization pits which have ceased to be able to produce coal on any tolerably economic basis have been closed. In recent years they have been closed under procedures agreed between the National Coal Board and the National Union of Mineworkers. Mr MacGregor has seen to it that these procedures have continued, but has added a vital new assurance, which is that every miner will be guaranteed a job in the industry if he wishes, or alternatively will be provided with an opportunity to take early retirement on terms more generous than any other industry in this country or in any coal industry in the world.

4 In your sermon you correctly draw attention to the adverse effect on a community if a pit is closed. I am perhaps more aware of that than even you are. In 1970 we inherited a situation where in the previous six years hundreds of pits had been closed. Indeed, pits had been closed at many times the rate of anything contemplated at the present time.

It was for this reason that I directed a great deal of environmental and economic aid to the North East between 1970 and 1974 – new roads, new homes, and new factories helped to bring new hope to the region.

In 1984 however the man whose departure you request became the first chairman of the National Coal Board to demand that the NCB themselves take on responsibility for any community affected by closure.

He has created a new company, providing aid, advisory services and accommodation to bring new firms and enterprises to the mining communities. The Government have undertaken to harness all the regional training and work experience programmes to support the activities of this new company. In reality, never previously has there been such a mobilization of finance and advice to help any mining community affected by a pit closure.

This at a time when the industry is not going to be devoid of investment, but when a massive investment programme is going to take place in the industry.

An examination of these four factors will show that there has never been a plan to defeat the miners. It is a plan I would certainly argue that deserves the support of any Christian, and is a plan to give miners and their families a better future than they have enjoyed in the past.

As a Christian I hope that in your moments of meditation and prayer you will ask why the 70 000 miners who were given a democratic vote, decided overwhelmingly not to strike. At such moments you could also ponder why it is that these men have day after day been threatened by mobs from outside their own communities. Mobs which have used violence and intimidation in order to prevent men who follow the normal traditions of the NUM from acting in accordance with the position of the majority of their colleagues.

I believe the reason why those miners who had the opportunity of balloting voted so overwhelmingly not to strike, and the reason why the other two-thirds of miners have been prevented from having a ballot, is because prior to this dispute we genuinely strived to create a position where there was a good wage offer, not a single compulsory redundancy, a massive investment programme and a positive programme for the mining communities.

In your sermon you stated 'that there must be no victory for the miners on present terms because this would mean pits left open at all costs and the endorsement of civil violence for group ends'. I do hope you recognize that this phrase explains the reason why miners have suffered so much for so long.

During this entire dispute Mr Scargill has not been interested in discussing the wages, the guarantee of no compulsory redundancies, the investment in the future or the offers prepared to assist mining communities. He has only made one demand and has only been willing to discuss one factor. This is the demand that any pit, no matter how uneconomic, should be kept open until the last tonne of coal is exhausted or until safety prevents the continuation of operations.

No miners' leader has ever made such a demand. No government and no National Coal Board management has ever or could ever concede such a demand. Mr Scargill has never moved or negotiated upon it. Whilst social democrats, moderate socialists, and trade union leaders all recognize that such a demand is unreasonable and unjustified, Mr Scargill has insisted that the non-balloted strike action shall continue until this demand is met.

Perhaps neither you nor I can analyse accurately his motives. But if you have embarked upon a study of Mr Scargill's written and spoken words over many years you can only come to the conclusion that he has always favoured conflict as opposed to participation, because he believes it is by conflict with the existing system that his utopia will be achieved.

Having stated in your sermon that you feel the necessity for Mr Scargill and the miners to move from this demand, can I perhaps ask you as a Christian bishop what you believe the Government or the nation should do if Mr Scargill continues, as he has for six months, to refuse to negotiate or to move from this demand?

You rightly stated in your sermon that anyone who

rejects compromise as a policy, programme or convention is putting himself or herself in the place of God. I know that both the Government and the National Coal Board have been eager and willing to pay the miners well, to free them from any risk of compulsory redundancy, and to help their communities invest in their future. This is not a case of putting ourselves before God, but of endeavouring to act in a civilized and Christian way.

You know and I know that Mr Scargill has been totally unwilling to move from his one unique and impossible demand.

As a person who has devoted most of his life to politics and to the Conservative Party, I have always believed that the correct tradition of my party has been to get the correct balance between efficiency and compassion. The trouble with compassion devoid of efficiency is that one never has the means of exercising the compassion. The trouble with efficiency devoid of compassion is that one creates a society so divisive that the efficiency itself is destroyed by the divisiveness of society. I cannot judge the degree to which I have succeeded in getting the balance correct on this particular issue. I do know that in my moments of meditation and prayer I have genuinely attempted to the best of my ability to understand the hopes and aspirations of miners and their communities. I have persuaded my Cabinet colleagues to devote considerable economic resources to see that their reasonable aspirations can be satisfied.

If I had considered that Mr MacGregor was a man who had either been instructed or personally had the intention of destroying the mining industry, or that he was contemptuous of miners or their communities, I would of course have dismissed him immediately. Or if it had been insisted that he had continued, I would certainly have resigned. But I know that Mr MacGregor is a man who wants this industry to succeed, who wants it to expand and not contract, and who has been eager to provide miners and their communities with aid and assurances never previously given under his predecessors. Perhaps your observations on Mr MacGregor were based upon his image as portrayed in propaganda rather than upon the genuine aspirations or faults of the man himself.

You and I agree that the miners must not be defeated. But we must do our best to assess who is the true enemy.

Peter Walker

From the Bishop of Durham, Auckland Castle
Bishop Auckland, Co. Durham DL14 7NR

28 September 1984

The Right Honourable P. Walker,
Secretary of State for Energy,
Thames House South,
Millbank,
LONDON SW1P 4QJ

Dear Mr Walker,
Thank you for your reasoned and informative letter of the 24th September. I greatly appreciate both the courtesy and the compassion you express. I am glad too of the opportunity for calm but urgent discussion between Christians about the frighteningly difficult problems which we all face, and about how our faith should interact with our practical and political decisions and stances.

The difficulties and differences between us seem to me to stem principally from two things. Firstly, I do not doubt your personal concern, nor your intentions, nor the value of many of the measures of which you write. Unfortunately, the government to which you belong does not *seem* to care for the steadily increasing number of people who are unemployed, and are otherwise marginalized in society, and does not seem to care that it does not seem to care. (You probably saw Mr Pym's gently cautious words on the subject in *The Times* of September the 19th in an article headed *Miners: Now for the Human Touch*).

On all the statistical tables known to me it seems a simple

matter of fact that this government's fiscal measures consistently improve the lot of (to use titles from one such table) 'senior managers' and 'company directors' while causing losses to 'jobless man with family' and 'semi-skilled worker'. This seems a gratuitous refusal to care and a rather insulting determination to make sure that the already under-privileged bear an even greater share of the cost of our undoubted economic difficulties, and of our undoubtedly required greater economic realism. It is also difficult to believe that the Government does care for all the members of our society when cuts are repeatedly made on those services which are of particular value to the poor, but money can always be found for military adventures in the Falklands, pretending to be still a great power in defence matters or keeping up the police forces. I do not say that we can do without either defence or police expenditure, but the emphasis does seem to be persistently on non-caring and aggressive directions.

This leads to the second principal point. I agree with you that Mr Scargill's personal intransigence has played and does play a very considerable part in keeping the situation over the mines deadlocked. I would guess that quite a few miners would like to see a situation rapidly developing in which they could do without Mr Scargill's intransigence. But it is necessary to ask why Mr Scargill gets the (by no means complete, but very strong) support that he does. The answer surely lies on the one hand in the general economic situation. Redundancy payments are all very well, and the redundancy arrangements of the NCB may well be the envy of threatened workers elsewhere, but redundancy means both no further jobs for the redundant, *and* no jobs for their children. Communities and a whole way of life are swept away at a time when there are no alternatives elsewhere. This is a vital difference between closing mines in the 60s and early 70s and closing them now. I am sure that many miners and their families remain doggedly committed to the strike not for money, but for a way of life. Whatever Mr Scargill may be after, they are seeking not revolution, but a future for something they have valued like life itself.

Then, on the other hand, Mr Scargill's intransigence is immensely reinforced by a government style which seems to make a virtue of confrontation. I had hoped, when I first drafted my Enthronement sermon two or three weeks before the event, that the page on the miners' strike could be either withdrawn or completely rewritten. But the Prime Minister's remarks on *The Jimmy Young Programme* reported in the papers of September the 20th convinced me that, with great sadness and perplexity, I could not alter a word. We seem to have intransigence confronted by intransigence, and this, I believe, is the death both of true politics and true community.

You yourself make a splendid point towards the end of your letter about compassion and efficiency. Of course, compassion does not get you very far in dealing with the problems of millions. We must have efficient production of the means of compassion. But surely this implies negotiating with and not destroying communities, groupings, and organizations which have grown up over the years, and which represent, however imperfectly, the legitimate aspirations and hopes of real and valued members of our society. It means developing a politics of the possible which carefully and compassionately considers the cost of any particular campaign in regard to the overall aims of the political struggle.

If the Government is really prepared to contemplate the pit strike going on for more than a year then it seems to me to have lost all sense of what a community is and what a country is. Something must be done speedily to stop communities tearing themselves apart, to stop bully boys in both mining pickets and police forces calling the tune, to stop ordinary families coming near to starving, and to stop the mining industry destroying itself. A government should be strong enough to be able temporarily to accept a compromise or check to its overall policies for the sake of local communities and particular persons. Such compromises would add to, not detract from, its authority.

You ask me what I would do if Mr Scargill continues to

refuse to negotiate on the one issue he says is not negotiable. I think I should challenge him to a 'cooling-off' period. Let both (?all) sides recognize the status quo at the moment. Where pits are effectively working leave them to work effectively, where pits are not working leave them not working – without either picketing to change the position or police to make sure that very small numbers of men have 'their right to work recognized'. Leave the communities around the pits alone, and let them make their own peace with local police and local miners. Meanwhile, resume all possible negotiations, using all parties that are available or willing, and abandon the pretence that it is a matter between the NCB and the workers, and not a government matter.

If the strike continues it is certain that miners, government and country will have been defeated. It is, therefore, surely, in the last analysis, up to the Government to consider what concession it can possibly make to break this dreadfully threatening deadlock, and free us all for further chances to tackle our problems without confrontation politics at every turn.

As you say, 'We must do our best to assess who is the true enemy'. I think that Christian insight would encourage us to recognize that *part* of the enemy is always within ourselves, and that no 'they', 'he' or 'she' should ever be treated as the total enemy, and the sole enemy. This does not make for simplicity of party slogans. But I think it does make for a compassion which if exercised politically might greatly add to efficiency and hope.

Yours sincerely,
David Dunelm

5 October 1984

The Rt Rev. the Lord Bishop of Durham
Auckland Castle
Bishop Auckland
County Durham
DL14 7NR

Dear Bishop,

Thank you for your reply to my letter. I appreciated your saying that my letter to you was reasoned and informative, and that you admired both the courtesy and the compassion which I expressed.

I appreciated this because it was certainly my intention to explain to you my sincere belief that both the National Coal Board and the Government have endeavoured, and are continuing to endeavour, to provide coal miners, their families and communities with a good future, and that they fully understand the miners' present problems.

I am sure your reply to me was intended to be what you described as 'an urgent discussion between Christians about the frighteningly difficult problems which we all face'.

I would like however to express my concern about some of the fundamental arguments in your letter.

Your prime argument is that the Government does not seem to care for the unemployed. The words 'not seem' are of course important. It may be a criticism of our failure to convey not just our concern but our actions to meet the problems of the unemployed.

I know of no problem which dominates more the thinking and the anxieties of both myself and the Government. As somebody whose father was an unemployed factory worker in the 1930s, there is nothing that I hate more passionately than the despair of unemployment. I must ask you to examine the range of measures that this Government is currently applying in order to relieve the burdens of unemployment created by the worst recession this century. Just let me list this year's expenditure upon government schemes designed to tackle this problem:–

Youth Training:– To provide training and planned work experience to enable school-leavers to compete more effectively in the labour market. £820 million

Young Workers' Scheme:– To encourage employers

to take on more young people into permanent full-time jobs. £56 million

Community Industry:– To provide temporary jobs for disadvantaged young people who find particular difficulty in finding and keeping jobs. £26 million

Enterprise Allowance:– To help unemployed people who wish to start up in business. £66 million

Community Programme:– To provide temporary jobs for the long-term unemployed of community benefit. £561 million

Full-time and Part-time Job Release:– To encourage employed people approaching state pension age to give up work early and release jobs for the unemployed. £315 million

Renovation of local authority housing £1005 million

Grants for private housing home improvements £450 million

The inner city urban programme dealing with the special concentration of social need for the inner city £255 million

Grants to eradicate derelict land £74 million

All this expenditure has been motivated by the desire to ease the problems of unemployment.

You go on in your letter to create the image of a nasty government, however, by claiming cuts in those services which are of particular value to the poor. A rather remarkable allegation against a government which in its first five years more than doubled expenditure on the health services in cash terms and substantially increased it in real terms, thereby allowing the numbers of nurses and doctors to be increased. An unfair allegation about a government which, during a world recession in which manufacturing production has been dramatically cut, so that the means of exercising compassion were reduced, decided that no old age pensioner suffered and kept its election pledge to protect pensioners from the ravages of inflation. To keep our word at a time when the gross national product in real terms was falling was, of course, a very considerable financial burden. Government expenditure on the elderly is now nearly £10 billion more per year than it was in the year before we came into office. We have more than doubled expenditure for the elderly in this period.

You seem in your letter to imply that there is something wrong in finding money for what you describe as military adventures in the Falklands. I hope I don't have to presume from this that, as an Anglican Bishop, you would have allowed the military adventures of the Fascist Junta in the Argentine to succeed, and the freedom of citizens for whom we had responsibility to be destroyed. As to your mention of the fact that we spent money on keeping up the police force, I can assure you that there are 70 000 people working in the coal industry who are very relieved we have done that.

What concerns me most about your letter and your sermon is the difference of your emphasis and attitude between Mr Ian MacGregor and Mr Arthur Scargill.

Mr MacGregor has offered the miners what everybody agrees to be a good pay offer, plus a guarantee that all miners will be able to continue working in the industry if they wish to do so, plus a massive investment programme in the future, plus a programme to bring new businesses to mining communities. For this Mr MacGregor is not just condemned but is chosen by you as the person who should be removed from office.

But Mr Scargill receives only an aside in your sermon to the effect that you hope Mr Scargill will not continue as an absolutist but become a compassionate and realistic negotiator who cares more for people and for their future than for an ideology. In your letter you merely describe Mr Scargill as having a personal intransigence.

Do let the public know in more detail how you really view Mr Scargill. I know you have made a considerable study of Marxist theory and practice. Where do you feel he fits into all of this? I am sure you have read his article in *Marxism Today* in which he displayed a Marxist contempt for democracy, and his article in *New Left Review* in which, referring to his mob successes at the Saltley coke depot, he wrote 'Here was the living proof that the working class had only to flex its muscles and it could bring Governments, employers, society to a total standstill'. What are your thoughts on this?

Do you feel that the writings, oratory and actions of Mr Scargill are just those of somebody displaying a degree of personal intransigence, or do you feel that they are the actions of somebody on a political crusade which is contrary to the desires of the majority of the people in our country? I posed to you the important question – what if Mr Scargill continued to go for conflict and adhered to a demand that he knew that neither Government nor the National Coal Board could ever agree to? Your reply to that question was remarkable. You replied you would go for a cooling off period in which pits not working would continue not to work and working pits would continue to operate. The strike would continue, without the pickets. But I must ask you, as a Christian and as a Bishop – why do you think Mr Scargill keeps up the mass picketing? Why does he ignore the guidelines of the TUC, and his own union, that only 6 peaceful pickets can operate at any colliery entrance? Why have there been 7000 arrests on criminal charges? Why are there victimization and beatings up on a massive scale? And why has Mr Scargill never on any occasion appealed for violence by the picket mobs to stop? There would be no need for police if Mr Scargill abided by the guidelines of his own union on picketing but of course what there would be would be a massive return to work of miners that have been deprived of a ballot.

You argue in one passage of your letter that Mr Scargill has very strong support – seemingly never strong enough to ballot his members, seemingly never strong enough to rely on the peaceful picket as opposed to the mass mob.

You go on to argue that redundancy payments are all very well but redundancy means no further jobs for the redundant and no jobs for their children.

You must look at the facts. What the Coal Board is primarily offering is for men in their 50s early retirement on generous terms. I am sure you would agree that at a time of unemployment, early retirement on generous terms is a strong assistance in that battle. As to your argument that the retention of a totally uneconomic pit is important to provide jobs for their children, it is a proposal that does not stand up to examination. Virtually all of the pits that we describe as uneconomic now, the 10 per cent of the pits that are losing £300 million a year and producing coal that costs way above the average costs of production, are virtually all pits that, even if you continued this waste of resources, would be exhausted of coal long before the children were able to obtain jobs at them. And even if they could last, you would be condemning tomorrow's teenagers to a working life deep in the ground in the most dangerous and uncomfortable of our pits. I cannot believe that it is Christian charity to preserve these sort of jobs when, economically, there is no need.

How much better instead of wasting such resources to provide new resources to bring in new firms, new enterprises and new industry into the mining communities where pit closures are going to take place. Mr MacGregor is the first chairman of the National Coal Board to take a decision to provide finance and services to see that that is done. This is a real long-term method of aiding the communities. The retention of an uneconomic pit has no such advantage.

As a Christian bishop in a mining diocese your objectives must be identical to the policies that the Government are willing to finance. A mining industry that can pay its miners well; a mining industry taking decisions that will give it an expanding and not a contracting future; and a mining industry meeting its responsibilities to see that when a pit can no longer produce coal on a sane and sensible basis that community is provided with generous provisions to encourage new enterprises. Guarantees that any person wishing to continue as a miner elsewhere is able to do so.

What as a Christian bishop you must not do is to encourage the belief that if miners are deprived of the right to ballot and, if mob rule and violence are imposed then demands devoid of logic and sanity will have to be fulfilled.

Daily I receive by letter appeals from those who are suffering from the violence and intimidation on a scale that neither you nor I have ever witnessed. Mr Len Murray spoke out against it. Mr Kinnock on two occasions has spoken out against it, although he cannot distinguish between the defensive action the police have to take and the offensive measures that the attackers have used. He treats the fire brigade with the same contempt as he treats the fire. In your sermon you mentioned, as an aside, that violence should not be rewarded. I do suggest to you that you could well preach to the miners leaders, and to Mr Scargill if he listens to preachers of your faith, that Christians would judge the cause to be sound if it was freely supported, and suspect it to be very unsound if force and intimidation have to be used.

What also depressed me about your letter was those matters raised in my original letter to you that you decided to ignore. I asked you why it was that Mr Scargill had decided for the first time in your lifetime to call a national strike in his industry without giving his members the right of a ballot.

I asked how you could accuse a Government that invested £650 million more in the coal industry than had been agreed under the 'Plan for Coal' which was endorsed by the Labour Government and the National Union of Mineworkers.

I asked you to express your appreciation of Mr MacGregor as the first chairman of the National Coal Board to demand that the National Coal Board themselves took on a responsibility for the future of the communities affected by closure.

I asked you as a Christian in your moments of meditation and prayer to ask why the 70 000 miners who were given a democratic vote, decided overwhelmingly not to strike and ponder why it is that these men have day after day been threatened by mobs outside their own communities.

I asked you if you did recognize that when in your sermon you stated 'That there must be no victory for the miners on present terms because this would mean pits left open at all costs and the endorsement of civil violence for group ends', you were in fact explaining the reason why miners, their families and their communities have suffered so much for so long.

It would be very difficult for any Christian bishop to suggest that what is being offered by the Coal Board and the Government to the miners and their communities was other than understanding, compassionate and decent.

Yours sincerely,
Peter Walker

4

Gorbachev and the Soviet Union

Throughout Peter Walker's political life foreign policy and defence policy of the United Kingdom has been dominated by the attitudes and potential dangers of the Soviet Union.

Walker has studied the Soviet scene as closely as any other contemporary politician. Both in the Heath Government and the Government of Mrs Thatcher he has carried out important negotiations in Moscow with Soviet leaders. Since Mr Gorbachev came to power he has twice visited the Soviet Union and spoken to a wider range of the new Soviet leaders. In 1984 Peter Walker had lengthy and absorbing discussions with Mr Gorbachev and realized then that this man would soon become leader of the Soviet Union and that if he did the Soviet Union would have a younger leader of high intelligence who would be personable in western terms. Having come to this conclusion Peter Walker has studied every action and pronouncement of the new Soviet leader. It is with this background that he wrote an essay with his analysis of the future impact of the Soviet Union under Gorbachev.

THE SOVIET UNION BETWEEN NOW AND THE NEXT CENTURY

Perhaps the most significant change in the international scene of the 1980s is the emergence of Mr Gorbachev as the leader of the Soviet Union. The Soviet Union presents the economic and the military alternative to the western democracies. The future of the massive expenditure by the Soviet Union as well as by Western Europe and the United States on defence will depend upon the attitudes of the Gorbachev Government in the coming decade. Economic relationships between the Soviet Union and the West will be dominated by the degree to which Mr Gorbachev succeeds in bringing real economic growth to the Soviet Union. The extensions of human freedom worldwide will depend very much on the attitudes of Mr Gorbachev.

I first met Mr Gorbachev in 1984 when he visited Britain, leading a high-powered group of Soviet officials and training experts with the purpose of trying to increase trade with the United Kingdom. At the time, however, it was speculated very strongly in the West that he could well be the next leader of the Soviet Union. If there was to be a generation change, Mr Gorbachev was probably the leading contender.

I found myself next to Mr Gorbachev at a dinner organized as part of his visit. For three hours we conversed together. They were for me an impressive three hours. I was greatly struck by the speed with which he reacted to any question or any argument. He was obviously a man of immense intelligence. If one studies his academic record in the Soviet Union one will find it is a record that any leading academic would be proud of. I naturally questioned him on the controversial issues of the day.

I particularly discussed with him the possibilities presented by a closer relationship between western capitalism and eastern communism in the years ahead. On these issues he took what one could anticipate to be the hardline Soviet view. He made no attempt to moderate his belief in the fundamental importance of the pure application of communism. But I was speaking to somebody whose future chances of the leadership depended at that moment on ensuring that no-one in the hierarchy of the Soviet Union was disturbed by his attitude or views. It was therefore unlikely that Mr Gorbachev would elaborate any new theories to a western politician about how the Soviet Union of the future could be different from the Soviet Union of the past.

He did, however, leave me with the very firm impression that if this man was to become leader of the Soviet Union, then the country would be led by a man of great drive, ability, and energy. There was nothing in my conversation with him which spelt out that he would pursue different objectives from Soviet leaders since the Revolution, but I felt that this might be a necessary façade for a man who stood on the threshold of power. I felt that behind those intelligent eyes and quick sense of humour, there might be a person who would decide to take the Soviet Union in a different direction. After my meeting I took an immense interest in all that Mr Gorbachev had done and all that he had said on the public record for I felt that the destiny of the world was likely to be substantially influenced by the future application of this thinking.

We should not be surprised that Gorbachev did become the leader of the Soviet Union. There is no doubt that the Soviet Union was becoming increasingly depressed at the manner in which it was falling behind the western world in living standards, as the productivity of its agriculture and its industry failed to match what was going on in most of Western Europe, United States and those areas in the Pacific Basin which operated under the free enterprise system. The Soviet Union was also depressed by the higher living standards and diversity of goods that were available in the more entrepreneurial eastern European countries. There was no doubt that Hungary and East Germany had devoted more attention to encouraging people to produce a diversity of consumer goods of a higher quality and were reaping the benefits of productivity greater than anything occurring throughout most of the Soviet Union. These indeed had been matters that had been discussed by Mr Gorbachev during his visit. For the Soviet Union to continue with a further period of elderly leadership, without thrust, energy or imagination would indeed have been a dangerous thing for them and perhaps also for the world at large. I wondered about the speed with which he would be able to make any inroads into the many fundamental problems which would face anyone wishing to change the direction of the Soviet Union.

The first problem would be to influence opinion in such a massive country as the Soviet Union, and to effect change across the fifteen separate republics which form the USSR. Each republic has its own political system and its own political leaders, many of them having a stronger sense of identity with their own republic than with the Soviet Union as a whole. In all of them there is a well established hierarchy, a well established bureaucracy and a well established KGB. Any change would need to be implemented against a range of different nations, different attitudes, different historic positions, and indeed different religious backgrounds.

Secondly there would be the immense difficulty of transforming the social and economic attitudes of a population that has had no other experience than that of the Soviet system. It is now nearly seventy years since any form of market mechanism was allowed to operate within the Soviet Union, and arguably even before Russian people never experienced real political freedom. This of course is a contrast to countries like Hungary and East Germany, and even countries like China where, within living memory, market forces and commercial activity have operated with enthusiasm and energy. There is nobody in the Soviet Union who can remember or recall such activities taking place. To introduce a change to a more market-orientated system would therefore be to eradicate the attitudes and prejudices of the past seventy years and replace them with new attitudes. This would be a difficult task at any moment in history but an even more difficult task given the fast fluctuations of the international market place today, and to do so in a nation which is so vast and is under such a massive bureaucracy as that of the Soviet Union.

Despite the daunting scale of the problem, Mr Gorbachev has made a whole range of very swift changes by Soviet standards. Many of the leading and elderly members of the Politburo have been retired. New and younger people have taken their places. Throughout the whole political system new, younger activists have been taking important and significant leadership positions.

The immediate result of their work and activities was expressed in the Twenty-Seventh Congress where Mr

Gorbachev set out very ambitious plans for the Soviet Union covering the period between now and the end of the century. If he succeeds with these plans, he will double Soviet production in fifteen years. He will improve the consumer standards of the Soviet people by a greater amount in those fifteen years than they have been improved in the last seventy years put together. He will give the Soviet Union an international presence in world trade, as both an importer and an exporter, on a scale that has never previously been contemplated by the Western union or indeed by the Western world.

What are the main motivations behind the personality of Mr Gorbachev? I believe that he has a very passionate and deep sense of patriotism. He is very proud of the Soviet Union. He has a deep desire for his country to succeed. He resents the fact that over the past decades the Soviet Union has failed compared with the West to apply high technology to its commerce and its industry. He resents the failure of Soviet agriculture. He abhors the incompetence and inefficiency of the vast bureaucracy. He believes that within the Soviet Union there is a combination of human talent and ability combined with vast material resources that should make it the most powerful and prosperous country in the world. His objective is quite simply to see that when the next century begins it begins with a Soviet Union that does not balance the United States and the western world merely in military strength but equals them, if not surpasses them, in economic performance. His speeches, his essays, his television addresses all bear witness to his passion to eradicate the gap between western and Soviet performance.

One of the words that enters his vocabulary more than most is 'discipline'. He is a man who, to achieve his rise to power, has of course applied considerable discipline and application to himself. Those whom he has brought to power are all men one can recognize as having disciplined themselves to apply their considerable abilities to the full. He therefore resents the spectacle of incompetence, lethargy, inefficiency and alcoholism. He feels that the Soviet Union has moved to a situation where bad performance goes unnoticed, dilatoriness and laziness are in no way prevented and indeed such weaknesses as massive alcoholism are affecting the whole momentum of the Soviet state.

In his very earliest days he launched a campaign against the Soviet people's massive indulgence in alcohol. The problem of alcohol abuse has meant that the Soviet Union is almost alone of developed countries in having a declining expectancy of life, from sixty-eight to sixty-one for the Soviet male in the last twenty years for example. A short time after coming to power he laid down that all of those involved in official entertaining must eradicate the alcohol content. A major banquet or lunch given by the Soviet Union is now an occasion about which the temperance movement would rejoice.

The Gorbachev attack on alcoholism has been accompanied by a similar attack upon bureaucracy. In Britain one modestly staffed Department of Energy is responsible for coal, gas, electricity, oil and nuclear industries. It is responsible too for the energy efficiency campaigns and the foreign trade pursuits within this sector. The Soviet Union has an Energy Bureau, a Ministry responsible for oil refining, another ministry for oil development, a ministry for gas, a ministry for coal, a ministry for power and electrification, and a ministry for nuclear power. It has another ministry responsible for the research and scientific applications, another responsible for the foreign trade applications, another for preparation of investment plans. A mass of correspondence takes place between all these ministries. Decisions are disputed and action is not taken. The Gorbachev approach to this is that the Communist party must now take a far more critical view of the bureaucracy. It must demand results and intervene to ensure that progress is made. Gorbachev also seems keen to open up a dialogue with his bureaucracy and increase accountability. The problems and frustrations of the development of the Soviet machinery industry, for example, resulted at an early stage in him placing a prominent person to be responsible for progress

– seeing that targets were reached and achieved in that industry.

A week or so before I arrived in Moscow a new Deputy Prime Minister was appointed to be head of the new Energy Bureau. The objective in establishing the Bureau was not that it should create policy; which was to continue to be the task of the Council of Ministers. The rôle of the Bureau was to ensure the full and efficient implementation of the Council's policy. The previous year was the first time Soviet oil production had dropped – not due to any lack of oil – but due to the incompetence and inefficiency of those conducting the business. The new Energy Bureau will have the task of seeing that the programmes are achieved across the whole energy field and the liveliest and ablest men are put in charge, replacing if necessary those who have displayed incompetence.

But perhaps the most interesting aspect of the Gorbachev change is his emphasis on the need to work, the need to work hard. He describes it as 'working in a disciplined manner' but he also recognizes the role of incentive if this task is to be achieved.

In Marxist theory the achievement of communism is said to be a two-stage process. The first phase, socialism, is based upon the principle of 'from each according to his ability, to each according to his work' resources will not be allocated by the principle 'from each according to his ability, to each according to his need' until the full communist state is arrived at. Gorbachev clearly emphasized in his first year in power the need to operate the socialist principle of allocating resources to each according to his work. Soviet agriculture has never attained anything like the results of western agriculture due to the total lack of incentive. The great collective farms have been given targets and if the targets were reached they were then raised. Soviet farmers never exceeded their targets because they received no reward other than having higher targets to achieve in the future. Mr Gorbachev now states that if the targets are achieved the surplus obtained above the targets can be sold in the market place and the proceeds go to the benefit of those operating the farms concerned.

Gorbachev has witnessed the manner in which Chinese agriculture has been totally reformed through inducements and incentives. Chinese food production soared when it moved from the communist principle of collective farms, with no disparity and reward, to more market-oriented principles. In addition the diversity of goods in the shops has been massively transformed and a new, tolerably wealthy class has been created. Mr Gorbachev is not moving as far as the Chinese moved, but to move at all towards a system of direct financial inducement and a market place for surplus foods to be sold is a very fundamental transformation which may well bring some dramatic results to the improvement of Soviet agriculture.

Gorbachev has also agreed to joint ventures with western companies in agriculture on a very considerable scale. For example ICI have been given great tracts of land to experiment with the application of their earth-advisory techniques, with the result that in certain locations where they have operated there has been a massive increase in the productivity of the wheat growers. If there is a transformation in Soviet cereal production it will of course have a major world impact. The United States has in recent years exported to the Soviet Union an average $2 billion of grain per year. United States farmers are already faced with the severe problems of disposing of their surplus production but nothing compared to the problems that will affect them if the Soviet Union achieves its potential as a grain producer. In such a case, the Soviet Union could not only eradicate imports from the US but could enter the market place itself as a major exporter.

Economic growth is the very essence of the Gorbachev policy. When he addressed the Twenty-Seventh Congress he made his position clear:

> 'There is no other way. In the absence of accelerated economic growth our social programmes will remain wishful thinking. In radical terms the main targets of

> this intensive development are that by the end of the century national income should nearly double, energy consumption per unit of output should drop by more than a quarter, better consumption per unit of output by nearly half, while labour productivity should nearly double. Throughout the period a major emphasis will be put on investment, modernization and greater efficiency and production. There is more than £200 billion in capital investment under the 1986–95 year plan with the accent upon new resources saving technologies, higher labour productivity and better quality.'

For Mr Gorbachev to succeed in his objective of the economic revival of the Soviet Union he knows that in the first place he will need a great deal of western technology. He will have to reach agreements with western powers for the exchange of scientific and technological information which will not be concluded in an atmosphere of hostility and friction between the West and the Soviet Union. If the Soviet Union is left without the ability to import technology and the new machinery and plants that are required for improving its industrial performance, the gap between the economic performance of the Soviet Union and the western world will increase and not narrow. On my visit to Moscow I recognized in the sphere of energy a whole range of areas where the Soviet Union would be anxious to secure our expertise.

Mr Gorbachev and his new technocratic colleagues in the Politburo intend to improve the quality and practical application of Soviet science and technology. The research potential of higher education is to be used more effectively and to this end there will be greater reliance upon material incentives for research collectives and individual researchers who make a real contribution to solving the problems of production.

The improvement of the consumer's lot is perhaps an objective for which Mr Gorbachev will be given greatest political support by the establishment of the Soviet Union as time goes on. The consumer standards of the Soviet Union are deplorably low. Moscow itself has a very narrow choice of food. There are frequently queues for food and always an appallingly bad diet. Long queues form when fundamentals such as shoes come into the shops. Many people in the Soviet Union know from their television screens or perhaps from visits to eastern Europe or the West, of the disparity in their consumer standards and those of other nations.

Despite his desire to see consumer standards rise, Gorbachev will not allow consumer demands to be met by imports. He does not have the hard currency with which to purchase them, and in any case his sense of patriotism leads him to believe that there is no need to import when the Soviet people have the ability, the talent, the raw materials to see that they produce them themselves.

For the observer of the Soviet scene the most fascinating factor of the next few years is the degree to which Mr Gorbachev will be able to give personal inducements and to see that the reality of the market place is recognized. He told the Twenty-Seventh Congress:

> 'Prices must be made more flexible. Price levels must be linked not only to outlays but also to the consumer properties of goods, their effectiveness and the degree to which products meet the needs of society and consumer demand.'

Individual economic enterprise is to be given more freedom to take its own commercial decisions. Major parts of Soviet industry are going to have their own direct accounting so that one can make a judgement on their effectiveness and performance. Gorbachev has promised that out of the results of that accounting those involved in producing good results will personally benefit.

Mr Gorbachev is the first Soviet leader to make perfectly clear the degree to which the improvement of the social conditions of the people is related to their economic performance. He has held out the prospect that if the economy improves in accordance with the scale he lays down it will instigate a plan to double the volume of resources allocated for the improvement of the conditions of life over the next fifteen years. He wishes to see real per capita incomes rise by between 60% and 80% but has pointed out that these plans will only become a reality if every Soviet person works hard and efficiently. He recognizes the hostility to the deplorable housing conditions in much of the Soviet Union and has stressed his desire to see a major improvement take place. He has pledged to provide every family with a house or flat of its own by the year 2000. He recognizes that in the Soviet Union at the present time one in four families is sharing accommodation with another family.

In the Gorbachev plan there is a great desire that all pupils should learn how to use computers and throughout the whole educational system he wishes to put a far greater emphasis upon the training of engineers and technicians. In health, greater emphasis is to be put upon preventive techniques and the maintenance of a more healthy life. 'Health cannot be bought in a pharmacy' was how he put it, and his campaign against drinking and alcoholism is an important contribution to this viewpoint.

There will undoubtedly be those of the old guard of the Soviet Union who feel that this is a fundamental assault upon the system laid down by Lenin and operated by the Soviet Union since the Revolution. There will also be those who will find that their rewards from having been part of a static bureaucracy will deteriorate relatively and they too will be opposed to such a change of system. The educational system and the propaganda of the teaching over these past sixty years will all operate against the recognition of the part that the market place has in objective decision making. It will be interesting to see the degree to which trade unions, limited as they are in power of any description, will take to the new system. It will be interesting to see that when the food that comes from the surpluses beyond the targets that have been given is priced at different prices from the basic food supplies; and the objections or the approval by the public at large to such radical changes.

Will Mr Gorbachev succeed? If he does succeed, what are the implications for the West? The likelihood is that he will neither succeed nor fail. He will achieve an improvement in the performance, but not of the dimension he anticipates and hopes for.

Mr Gorbachev shares the traditional Soviet anxiety about the development of nationalist and religious feelings in the various republics of the Soviet Union. He warned:

> 'Certain works of literature and art and scholarly writings were produced under the guise of national originality. Attempts are being made to depict in idyllic tones reactionary nationalist and religious revivals contrary to our ideology – the Socialist way of life and our scientific world outlook.'

In other words, he and his colleagues of the new Politburo seem no more likely to look kindly upon the aspirations of Moslems, Christians, Jews or decadent artists and intellectuals than any of their predecessors did. In all such cases, freedom of thought and expression remain the most disturbing challenges to the hold of the Communist party upon the hearts and minds of the Soviet people.

Recently in Moscow there have been suggestions that there has been greater freedom given to the theatre and to the films, but an analysis of this greater freedom shows that in many cases the objective was not to create a criticism of the Soviet position or a greater degree of freedom, but to allow a more subtle analysis of the horror and evil of capitalism.

This conformity of view is, however, somewhat challenged by Mr Gorbachev's desire to have what he describes as 'a further development of all the aspects and manifestations of Socialist democracy'.

Mr Gorbachev has indicated a desire for the Trade Union movement to be more forward looking, he has endeavoured to encourage increased participation in a flow of views from a more active trade union movement. Mr Gorbachev has argued, 'the Socialist system can develop successfully only when the people really run their own affairs, when millions of people are involved in political life'. But of course if millions of people were involved in political life they would, as is natural in the human race, have differences of viewpoint and some of those viewpoints would almost certainly be in stark contrast to the ideology propounded since the Revolution took place. The new leadership undoubtedly wants to initiate something close to a dialogue between people and government. It wishes to increase the influence of local political control over the bureaucracy and to overcome the administrative shortcomings which Mr Gorbachev has described as 'a departmental approach and localist irresponsibility, red tape and formal indifference to people'.

Mr Gorbachev undoubtedly wishes to see that all those in authority, at every level, and especially the party cadres encourage and respond to fuller participation in the elaboration, adoption and execution of official decisions. He wants to spread what he describes as 'the electivity principle' to all team leaders at work and subsequently to some other categories of management, since he believes this to be the best way of making a success of 'democratic centralism' in the Soviet Union. He also urges more publicity of decisions taken at all levels of administration on the grounds that 'without publicity there is not, nor can there be, democracy, political creativity by the citizen and participation in administration and management'.

Indeed quite extraordinarily he has even canvassed the possibility of introducing a new law to provide for the holding of national referenda on some major issues of policy. It will be staggering to see such referenda take place in which there would be a vigorous propounding of the issue to be put and a vigorous oppposition, with the government to be taking no view whatsoever other than a desire to carry out the people's choice.

One certain thing is that if Mr Gorbachev is to achieve his economic and social objectives it means that he must have fifteen years in which rearmament and foreign friction are not the dominant aspects of his government. One could therefore argue that this may well be a time when no matter what his long-term motives may be, he will wish to move resources from the military to the domestic, when he will wish to see that vast investment programmes go into not just the industries essential for military superiority, but go into those necessary for economic and consumer equality with the West.

Mr Gorbachev has been very active in communicating to the world at large his view that the Soviet Union has a great desire for disarmament, and that it is the Americans who are the war-mongering nation. Whether it be a much pre-advertised nuclear test in which the United States is invited to be in attendance or capitalization on actions by the American Government to try and prevent and curtail terrorism being launched from countries like Libya, every opportunity is used by Mr Gorbachev to present each incident to the Soviet people as an example of American militarism and Soviet desire for peace.

In foreign policy Mr Gorbachev set out his ultimate objective in his statement of 15th January, 1986. It was a statement in which he asked for the abolition of all weapons of mass destruction by the end of the century. This is almost certainly a position adopted for rhetorical and propaganda purposes.

But Mr Gorbachev has also maintained that it is inspired by certain important principles and considerations. The first of these, he argued, is that the scale and destruction of modern nuclear weaponry effectively rules out any hope of safeguarding national security solely by military or technical means. The second is that the relations between the Soviet Union and the United States must be based upon mutual and universal security. The third is that the two superpowers, in his own words, 'have quite a few points of coincidence' and that 'there is the objective need to limit peace with each other, and to cooperate on a basis of equality and mutual benefit. There is no other basis.' The fourth is that the maintenance of a perpetual status quo is no longer possible while equally it is no longer possible to think in terms of winning an arms race or a nuclear war. Thus he maintained that 'The confrontation between capitalism and socialism can proceed only and exclusively in forms of peaceful competition and peaceful contest.'

Mr Gorbachev stressed the unilateral steps towards disarmament which have been taken by the Soviet Union, particularly the moratorium on the deployment of intermediate range missiles in Europe (a moratorium imposed of course after the advantage had been given to the Soviet Union).

He repeated the familiar assertion that Soviet military doctrine is unequivocably defensive and the Soviet Union will not be the first to use nuclear weapons. Of course he has always expressed his strong opposition to the development of the Star Wars technology too. This is an area where the Soviet Union is aware that the United States is well ahead on research and development and therefore it is important to him to see that it does not continue to develop.

What is significant, however, is that many will judge that Mr Gorbachev, although conceding nothing which in any way decreases the relative strength of the Soviet Union, has created an atmosphere in which it seems that he is the person desiring peace and the Americans the nation who are not taking the appropriate action. It is easy for him to proclaim a moratorium on the deployment of intermediate range missiles when his are in place and his opponents are not. It is easy for him to condemn Star Wars when he is secretly carrying out such a programme himself. It is easy for him to suggest a unilateral ban on nuclear tests when he knows that future nuclear tests have no significant importance to his own defence programme and when the tests are being carried out by his opponent.

But in fact no matter how weak the arguments are on examination they represent a major propaganda opportunity for the newly media-conscious Russians to present directly to western electorates, something which western leaders cannot of course do in the Soviet Union.

The West must never lose sight of the dominance of the Soviet Union in conventional weapons. Perhaps one of the ugliest and most worrying aspects of this dominance is its considerable armoury of chemical weapons. It is remarkable that within the European sector the Soviet Union have available to them some of the most appalling and terrible chemical weapons known to man, weapons that when used could stop all activity in or around the locations in which they are used, not just at the moment the weapons are used but for a considerable time thereafter. Whole areas of military operation could be neutralized for many days as a result of the use of these weapons.

If the world is to move from the constant threat of destruction to an era of peace and security, there is no doubt about the need for tough negotiations to take place to obtain internationally controlled disarmament. It is a combination of the nuclear and the conventional, particularly the chemical that needs to be on the top of the agenda for without it the balance of power would undoubtedly go to the Soviet Union.

In his worldwide relationships there is no doubt the most embarrassing issue is human rights. Mr Gorbachev has used some words about reuniting families, 'in a humane and positive spirit' and has called for round table discussions between the five permanent members of the United Nations Security Council. But the Soviet Union holds on to the view that it ought to be possible to 'make peaceful co-existence the highest principle of the state to state relationships'. In reality there are aggrieved minorities in the Soviet Union. There are people who are devoid of human rights.

Within the fifteen-year timescale of Mr Gorbachev's plan there are some very significant problems which he is going to have to face. The first problem is that if the Soviet Union does become more efficient and productive and applies modern technology it may create a significant amount of technological unemployment in a political system which does not recognize the existence of unemployment and which indeed stigmatizes unemployment as illegal. Mr Gorbachev estimated that the fundamental restoration of the national economy would produce annual savings of the equivalent of the labour of about twelve million people or of a hundred million tons of fuel and many billions of rubles.

This would be a considerable achievement if it could be attained – but what would happen to the twelve million displaced work people? Would they be absorbed into other efficient activities to the benefit of the economy as a whole or would they merely join the considerable number of under employed who already exist in the less efficient sectors? Visit any Soviet factory, any Soviet retail organization, any Soviet office and you see more over-manning and more people doing very little than exists in most places in the western world. Mr Gorbachev's demands for higher discipline, greater efficiency and more investment in high technology could in fact create either vast areas of over-manning and unbelievable inefficiency to the benefit of those who were not allowed to pursue such standards or alternatively a substantial number of people during a particular timescale who could not be given any useful employment.

Secondly, what is going to be the effect of the widening pay differentials necessary to provide extra material incentives and rewards for those with essential skills working in the most efficient sectors? These may not be acceptable to other Soviet workers who are not so fortunate and they may be difficult to reconcile convincingly with the original Marxist doctrine from each according to his ability, to each according to his need. The hard-nosed market approach will have difficulty in co-existing with the residue idealism of Soviet Socialism and there are indications in a number of areas where the old guard who had adhered very strictly to the original ideals of the communist state are showing a considerable hostility to the Gorbachev moves.

What for example is going to happen to the food market when suddenly there is a free food market with higher prices? Will those who cannot afford the higher prices decide to demand a change and a destruction of the system and a return to a system where everybody is on a target, is expected to meet the target and for meeting it to receive no reward other than a higher target?

Hungary has managed to use a semi-capitalist system without using any of the rhetoric of the capitalist system. In 1973 one of the leading Hungarian ministers explained to me how they had set out the national plan. Targets would increase for every individual firm, but they would be rather modest targets because they would be based upon the figures provided by the firms concerned, all of whom wanted to have no difficulty in reaching them. The Hungarian Government said to the Hungarian firms: if you beat your targets, part of the financial benefits will go to the workers, and a proportion to the state, but a very major proportion will go to the management. The proportions that were involved meant that the financial reward being offered to Hungarian managements was better than the rewards offered to British management.

I pointed out to the Hungarian Minister that he was creating a system more capitalist than the capitalist system. He replied that the result had been a great deal of vitality in the Hungarian economy and a far better consumer standard for Hungarian people than exists in the Soviet Union.

It is one thing for a country as small as Hungary with recent memories of the capitalist system at work to return to that system, be it disguised with the rhetoric of communism. It is a totally different principle for the country which was the very foundation of the Revolution and has operated a different system for seventy years to start making moves to a more competitively rewarded system and if those who feel that they are in any way handicapped shout the loudest, the political atmosphere may well be one of hostility towards such a concept.

How will Mr Gorbachev cope with the emerging problems of the different nationalities in the Soviet Union? There are significant disparities in the industrial performance and economic development of the fifteen republics. Will he move to penalize the recalcitrant and discriminate in favour of areas like Siberia and the Far East where progress is far faster? This sort of interference in the Soviet Union was practised successfully and brutally in Stalin's time but it is by no means certain that Mr Gorbachev has either the will or the capacity to emulate his tyrannical predecessor. What happens when it becomes all too apparent that the fruits of Soviet development and prosperity cannot be shared equally between the different republics and the various ethnic groups? Will the Moslems in the south turn anti-Socialist? Will the Ukraine continue to accept a sub-optimal economic performance as a price for supporting the poor republics? Will the Baltic republics of Lithuania, Estonia and Latvia be immune from the influences of Swedish television and British tourists? These problems, and nationality and regional problems, are probably containable but it is still worth remembering that the Soviet Union is an artificial creation of fifteen very different republics and it is fair to describe it as the last of the great European Empires.

In calling for closer supervision of officialdom at every level by the elected representatives of the people and for wider publicity and more participation in the interests of 'socialist democracy' Mr Gorbachev is really calling for an approach which has some similarity with Mao Tse-tung's Cultural Revolution. Those who know the Soviet Union well will recognize the hostility to such an approach which will come from such a conservative country. It will be interesting to see if the forces of inertia and reversion are as powerful in the Soviet Union as they proved to be in China.

The final difficulty if Mr Gorbachev deems that it is essential to make some major movement from military to economic and peaceful expenditure, will be in the degree to which this will be resisted. The Soviet Union with its experiences of the last war has genuine fears of a potential aggressor. Years of propaganda based upon an established view of the imperial West mean that the fear of aggression by the Soviet people from the West is a genuinely and sincerely held fear. It is impossible to relate to them the realities that democracies have no desire for war and have every desire to enjoy improving living standards rather than living standards threatened by the allocations of vital resources for a wartime machine. But the basic inherent fear of the Soviet people of aggression coupled perhaps with some basic feeling that the extension of communism to the world at large requires military strength will mean that in the hierarchies of the Soviet Union and in the hierarchies of the party itself there will be considerable debate of this issue.

The task of the West is to analyse the risks. Firstly, if disarmament can be negotiated in a genuinely balanced way under genuine international control, the release of resources devoted to the military for other purposes would be of immense advantage to the West and western democratic leaders in solving their economic and social problems. Secondly, if the Soviet Union were to achieve the rate of expansion it has in mind it would provide a general expansion in the world economy which would be a very considerable stimulant to world economic activity and undoubtedly a contribution to solving the problems of unemployment in the West as well as securing full employment in the communist-dominated East. It would be the new technology and new products of the West that would be in demand. Existing western exports of grain would no longer be required. A dramatic change in the nature of Western–Soviet Trade.

There is no doubt at all that in the minds of the new Soviet leadership an improvement of the Soviet image in the West is a major goal which if achieved could have a considerable effect upon western public opinion. If by efforts and individual inducement, or tougher discipline, or the purchase of higher technology higher levels of economic efficiency can be obtained they will have considerable impact upon the West. For example it is now possible for Lada Motors, from the Fiat-built assembly plant in the Ukraine, to manufacture and sell family saloon cars in Britain for about £3000 each. If this sort of competitive ability were to be extended to other sectors it might prove a severe threat or at least a commercial embarrassment to western producers with competing goods.

Obviously a great deal would depend upon the trade and tariff régime maintained by Great Britain and the European Community as a whole, yet assuming relatively low common external tariffs, a more efficient and competitive Soviet economy might offer new competition both in our own domestic market and in third markets as well as a new opportunity to our exporters.

When in 1973 I negotiated with several Soviet Ministers I was struck firstly by their age, and secondly the feeling that they were unable to be decisive when dealing with a foreigner. At the time I agreed a number of areas where we could investigate the possibility of collaboration both in research and in trade. I found on leaving Moscow it was almost impossible to make any progress and seemingly correspondence got lost in the general bureaucracy.

In my more recent dealings with Moscow the atmosphere has very much changed. The new Ministers appointed by Gorbachev are younger and brighter and have an eagerness to take action.

When I went to Moscow in April 1986 my host was the Chairman of the State Committee for Science and Technology and a Deputy Prime Minister, Mr Marchuk. He is a dynamic personality, a distinguished scientist, and a man who totally shares Mr Gorbachev's objective of seeing that the scientific skills of the Soviet Union are better harnessed to make economic and industrial progress.

Our meetings were decisive. We agreed a programme of work for the coming months. We agreed to monitor with each other the progress that was being made and to meet every half year and review the scene. In the months since then real progress has been made to the benefit of trade between the two nations.

Mr Marchuk has now been made President of the Academy of Sciences. This is a very powerful position in the Soviet Union as it makes him responsible for all major scientific institutions throughout the nation. He is heading the drive to make better use of the Soviet Union's substantial scientific skills.

In April I also met the new person to be in charge of energy in the Soviet Union. He was another Deputy Prime Minister, Mr Scherbina. His office is in the Kremlin but a few yards from that of Mr Gorbachev. He has the task of seeing that all of the energy industries meet their targets and has considerable power of intervention in any industry that is failing. He is a person with a strong personality, a good sense of humour, but again a person who is more interested in action than in words.

When the tragedy of Chernobyl took place it was Mr Scherbina who was immediately put in charge of all operations. Having discussed nuclear and other energy matters with Mr Scherbina in Moscow but a week before the Chernobyl incident I immediately contacted him to offer my sympathy and any help we could give. We were able to give a little help in the form of protective clothing. Mr Scherbina mobilized all that was available in the Soviet Union to meet the task. He organized the evacuation of 100 000 people. He organized the cleaning up of the remainder of the power station and the surrounding towns.

It was he who ordered that every fact should be disclosed to the International Agency. I pressed him to do this but I could not be confident that there would be an admission as to the faulty design of the Chernobyl reactors. Not only was there the fullest disclosure of all the human errors but also of the design and engineering errors and experts from throughout the world were given the opportunity of cross-examining the Soviet experts upon these issues.

I dined with Mr Scherbina the night before the meeting of the International Agency in Vienna and expressed my gratitude to him for the policy of full disclosure. I agreed with him what were the necessary measures to improve international safety standards. It was that evening that Mr Scherbina extended to me an invitation to come and see Chernobyl for myself. He said it would be a month or two before the other reactors were back in operation at

Chernobyl but as soon as they were he would like me to go and see for myself. It was the type of invitation that would not have come from the Soviet Ministers in the pre-Gorbachev period.

On 17th December 1986 I was the first person who was not a Soviet citizen to visit Chernobyl, to see for myself what had occurred and to be shown what had been achieved since the disaster took place.

The temperature was 28° below freezing. I flew in a ministerial jet from Moscow to Kiev accompanied by Mr Lunkonin, the newly appointed Minister of Nuclear Power. He is a man who has a background of nuclear engineering, who had been in charge of several of the Soviet Union's major nuclear installations, a man who was appalled at the managerial inefficiency that had taken place at Chernobyl, but a man dedicated in his view that the Soviet Union must massively increase the availability of nuclear power. On arrival at Kiev we had a quick early lunch with the leading political figures of the Ukraine and forty minutes later departed in a helicopter for the fifty-minute flight to Chernobyl.

It was depressing to fly over the deserted villages and townships near to Chernobyl which had been evacuated, to fly over Chernobyl itself and to see a small town in which there was no longer any sign of life apart from the activity at the power station itself.

The power station was on a major site where four nuclear reactors had previously been at work and two more were under construction. Less than seven months after the Chernobyl accident the reactor that had exploded was turned into a permanent concrete block. Two of the adjoining reactors were back at work, one in full operation and the other soon to be so, and the third going through its decontamination processes in order that it would be in full operation during 1987. We flew over the site in order that I could see from the air the location of the reactors and see the concrete containment of the offending reactor from the air as well as from the ground. We landed and were met by the new Manager of Chernobyl and his assistant. They took me to their offices and gave me a visual display that described in detail what had taken place and the measures that had been taken to deal with the gigantic problem of an exploded nuclear reactor.

They confirmed that the design of the reactor had been wrong, that there had been mistakes in the engineering and construction of the reactor and finally the mismanagement of the human beings who had been involved in disastrous and unauthorized experiments.

Unlike any western reactor there was no automatic device that eradicated human errors. There was no independent nuclear inspectorate. Unlike western reactors there were features of the building such as a roof that could easily catch fire; there was no sprinkler system for fire prevention for this type of reactor. These matters were now being remedied and at a gigantic cost, a cost equal to 12% of the cost of electricity in the Soviet Union.

What was impressive was the speed with which the problem had been contained. Using machinery that they had used to explore the moon they had put a frame around the offending reactor by remote control and then filled the frame with thousands of tons of concrete. They had tunnelled under the reactor with brave miners and laid a new foundation of concrete and lead beneath it. They had fitted instrumentation so that they could ascertain what was going on within this permanent concrete block.

The radiation had been eliminated and they then moved to the massive clearing up procedures.

It is these procedures that had enabled two of the adjoining reactors to be in operation already. New floors, new ceilings, the stripping and cleaning of every piece of machinery had moved the radiation levels down to below the safety levels required. The top one and a half inches of surrounding earth surface had been removed.

3500 men are now working at Chernobyl in safety, two weeks on and one week off, and in the one week off work they can join their families evacuated to Kiev. A new town was being built in which the families of those who operate

Chernobyl in the future would be able to live some miles from the site but by Soviet standards in attractive rural surroundings. The two reactors under construction were to be completed with work starting in the middle of 1987.

Chernobyl created for the Soviet Union an awareness of the necessity for safety standards of the highest order. I have little doubt with their skill in engineering and science they will at some cost achieve this.

The Soviet Union have no doubt that safety can and must be achieved in order that a substantial expansion, indeed a doubling, of nuclear energy can speedily be achieved.

The following day I was given lunch at the Kremlin by Mr Scherbina. There can be few occasions when a western Cabinet Minister in charge of but one department is given lunch by two Deputy Prime Ministers and six other Soviet Ministers. Without exception they were men younger than would have been the case a few years ago, competent and able and with a determination to meet Mr Gorbachev's demand to substantially improve the Soviet Union's industrial performance.

Changes are taking place. A minor measure in practice perhaps but an enormous measure in principle, is the legislation to allow the emergence of the private business, be it at this moment confined to the scale of the family.

A measure to allow joint ventures to take place between Soviet organizations and capitalist companies, a measure that Mr Gorbachev recognizes as essential if the Soviet Union is to start to catch up with western technology and industrial processes.

The increasing addiction to the view that it is the reward for work rather than meeting the need of the individual that is becoming the predominant aspect of Soviet economic thinking.

If these moves succeed the West must appreciate the dimension of the change in the world economic scene. The Soviet Union possesses 30% of the world's qualified scientists. If those 30% are applying their minds more and more to industrial success in an age of technology this will make the most enormous impact upon world economic activity.

We should remember that a young Soviet's chance of receiving a university education is almost twice as high as that of his British or West German counterpart.

In the 1939–45 war twenty million were killed in the Soviet Union and of the male babies born between 1920–25 only 3% survived. The Soviet Union therefore had a post-war tragedy in terms of the loss of young ability unparalleled in western Europe. But they now have an increasingly qualified and larger younger generation coming into positions where they can apply their ability.

In agriculture alone there is every potential that in a few years with the application of modern techniques the Soviet Union will cease to be the one remaining great importer of cereals with dramatic economic repercussions on both the United States and the European Community. That is but a beginning of what could happen in a whole range of consumer goods.

In his worldwide relationships Mr Gorbachev is well aware that the issue of human rights is an embarrassing one, which creates a great deal of anti-Soviet hostility. In his speeches he uses some words about reuniting families 'in a humane and positive spirit'. He has called for round-table discussions between the five permanent members of the United Nations Security Council.

Mr Gorbachev has made a number of significant decisions in releasing some of the more famous personalities who have been the subject of human rights campaigns. He has always done this quietly devoid of comment but has managed by a few well publicized releases to create an atmosphere in the West that he is more understanding and tolerant than his predecessors. This will, however, be one of the main continuing problems of the Gorbachev years. There are substantial aggrieved minorities in the Soviet Union. There are many people whose freedom has been almost totally eradicated due to their individual beliefs and background. If Mr Gorbachev succeeds in his campaign to bring a greater degree of democracy to the Communist party itself, to the trade unions and to the media, those almost totally deprived of their human rights will be in even starker contrast both within the Soviet Union and obviously within the wider concepts of the western democracies. The coming years will show whether Mr Gorbachev will encourage an exodus of large numbers of Soviet citizens currently enslaved or whether he will endeavour to cope by means of the regular release of the more internationally known personalities. Whichever course he pursues will be an important factor in the image of the Soviet Union that he is able to create throughout the world.

The leaders of the developing and emerging nations of the world are able to see the contrast in performance, the production and the performance in living standards between the Soviet system and the free enterprise systems of the West. There is no doubt at all that the standard of living of the ordinary person in the countries of western Europe, the United States and Japan is superior to that of the Soviet Union, that the consumer standards are deplorably low. But a Soviet Union that was performing better and was fast improving consumer standards, that was providing a quality of life that became more and more equal with the West would be a much greater political rival in obtaining the genuine support of third world countries. It could be pointed out by the West that the only reason for the Soviet success was that they were beginning to move towards the principles of the western democracies and away from the principles laid down in the Revolution.

The successful and comprehensive development of the Soviet economy along the lines set out by Mr Gorbachev would have the effect of making the Soviet Union a more complete and hence more formidable superpower adversary for the United States. Instead of being like a table with only one leg – military capability – the Soviet Union would look increasingly like a strong and well balanced piece of furniture with political, economic and cultural capabilities which would compliment and reinforce each other. Paradoxically this would make the Soviet Union into an even more formidable adversary but also a more self-assured and reliable partner for the western world, since her leaders would presumably no longer suffer from their traditional sense of insecurity and from the inferiority complex which in the past has sometimes worked against the interests of world peace.

What is certain is that if Mr Gorbachev retains the leadership of the Soviet Union between now and the end of the century it is likely that his policies and the policies of those men of ability with whom he has surrounded himself will have a gigantic impact upon world history. We will be faced with fifteen years holding within them enormous upside benefits for mankind or the ultimate downside risk of nuclear war.

It could be a period of a massive improvement in the performance of the Soviet economy with all the world-wide impacts that would have. It could be a period of genuine search for multilateral disarmament with all of the impact for good that would have. It could be a period of an easing of the dictatorial nature of Soviet communism and movement towards a society with greater freedom of expression and greater freedom of the individual. If any of these potentialities can be drawn out by western understanding and collaboration we should realize that it is certainly in the interests of the world that they are achieved. It could, however, be a period in which a more efficient and strong leader could ruthlessly pursue the objective of his predecessors – for Soviet communism to dominate the world – and to achieve that objective by the added strength which improved efficiency would provide. A system that would take advantage of the democratic pressure for disarmament and thus widen the gap between the military might of the Soviet Union and the military power of the western democracies.

It is the task of western statesmanship to identify whether the trends are for good or for evil, to give every encouragement if they are for good and to prepare every defence if they are for evil.

5

The Next Fifteen Years

In the previous chapter Peter Walker assessed how the Soviet Union might tackle its enormous problems in the decade to come. He saw scope for a huge improvement in the Soviet economy; a great rise in standards for Russian consumers; and the risks and opportunities the Kremlin's new leadership would mean for the West.

In a speech in Worcester, he expressed the need for the European Community to grasp its political and economic opportunities.

THE EUROPEAN OPPORTUNITY

To any schoolboy of the 1940s the supremacy of Europe in world affairs was simply taken for granted. We were conscious of the power of the United States; we argued about the morality of colonialism. But the fact that Hitler's aggression caused a world war, rather than another in the long line of European wars, didn't seem odd; we wouldn't have expected anything else.

Yet we can now see that within a quarter of a century from the end of the Second World War, Europe clearly lost the world leadership role she had enjoyed for 300 years. What had seemed in our school days to be permanent and inevitable turned out to be a phase of history that was drawing rapidly to its close.

The decline in the importance of Europe in the post-war years can be measured in a number of ways. Military leadership clearly passed to the Soviet Union and the United States, and the peace of Europe was underwritten by the formation of NATO and the Warsaw Pact, based on military leadership from outside the continent. Despite the successful rebuilding of the European economy, European living standards fell behind those prevailing in the United States, and more recently behind those in Japan as well. Within the United States, attention increasingly shifted towards the Pacific seaboard, and away from the more European East Coast establishment. Even in the arts, questions have been raised about the vitality of the traditional artistic centres in Europe, and American and – more recently – Japanese centres have attracted talented performers and critical acclaim.

Furthermore, if Europe has been eclipsed by North America and Japan all three regions now face new challenges from the emerging countries South America and south and south-east Asia. The countries of Asia and the Indian subcontinent, together with South America, pose a competitive threat to the economic and cultural leadership of Japan and the United States similar to the threat they themselves earlier posed to the established centres of Europe.

In short, the stable, settled world picture of the inter-war years has gone for ever. Europe has already been toppled from its pedestal. Its position in the world, and with it the well-being of the Europeans, will henceforth depend on performance in a competitive world, in which the number of competitors is growing all the time. Most critically it will depend on the ability of the Europeans to ensure that their economies can compete successfully in the international market place, for in the world of the twenty-first century we shall find that the views of a Europe that is sliding quietly into genteel poverty will count for little.

The Europeans are collectively the heirs to a great inheritance. If we have the will and wisdom to use it, the world is full of opportunities; if, by contrast, we resolve to 'live on capital' we shall rightly simply earn the contempt of both our contemporaries and successors, and we shall find that a squandered inheritance doesn't last very long.

To allow the European economy to compete successfully in the world of the 1990s and beyond will require a leap of political imagination for which the governments of Europe are singularly ill-prepared. With a population of 320 million compared with 220 million in the United States and 120 million in mainland Japan, Europe should have many advantages. Yet despite the fact that the total European market is larger than either the US or Japan, no European company can think in those terms, as the markets of Europe remain fragmented.

Governments pay lip-service to the idea of a 'common market', and have made some progress towards dismantling the most obvious barriers to trade; yet regulatory agencies remain stubbornly nationalistic in outlook, and many official policies direct competitive effort towards national prestige or short-term political gain, rather than the long-term competitive threat from outside Europe.

For many businesses this doesn't matter. The fashionable political cause of the 1980s is the small business, and since these enterprises are – by definition – of limited scale, they can compete happily in markets the size of a European country without incurring any penalty as a result of a limited market. European countries neglected their small business sectors in the 1950s and 1960s; that neglect has now been reversed, and the benefits of a vigorous small business sector are starting to be felt.

The mistake many Europeans make, however, is to imagine that small businesses are the whole answer to Europe's economic problem. That is untrue. Europe's increasing weakness in the face of competition from Japan and the United States does not lie principally in the products of the small business sector – it lies in major strategic companies which are developing and then mass producing manufactured goods. It is Japan's strength in the motor industry, consumer electrical goods, optical goods and the like which create the trade imbalance between Europe and Japan, and which cannot be reversed by small business. The fragmentation of Europe has made it more difficult for the European response to the Japanese world-beater company to emerge, and it is to this weakness that the governments of Europe must now address themselves.

The most obvious field where official attitudes have to change concerns competition policy. It is clearly absurd for governments to talk of 'completing the internal market' while at the same time leaving intact anti-trust machinery which measures monopoly market shares by reference to national markets. The result is that Europe has up to fifteen major motor companies against three in the USA, five in Japan. If we are serious – as we must be – about creating a single market in Europe, then the market must be regulated by a single community agency which will, like any other anti-trust body, be interested in local monopolies, but which will be principally concerned with promoting healthy competition on a continental scale, among companies able to compete on a worldwide basis.

It is now over ten years since the governments of Europe formally committed themselves to the objective of 'Economic and Monetary Union'. This is the most fundamental step towards the creation of a single competitive market in Europe, for until a manufacturer knows for certain how many francs he will receive for goods produced in France and sold in Germany the national frontier will always remain a significant barrier to trade. It is often argued that this uncertainty can be hedged on the foreign exchange markets. In the very short term that is true, but it doesn't help a manufacturer decide whether to commit himself to an investment decision that may have a life of twenty years. Similarly, the EMS – although a timid step in the right direction which has certainly reduced exchange rate fluctuations – deals only with the symptoms of the problem, rather than its cause.

Exchange rate stability will not dawn in Europe until the goal of 'Economic and Monetary Union' becomes a reality. If the monetary authorities in the member states pursue different monetary policies, exchange rate fluctuations are inevitable. The leaders of Europe must therefore now return to their commitment to economic and monetary union and take the steps necessary to create a single European currency, with the necessary institutions to manage a European monetary policy. The creation of a monetary union is a goal for the next decade as important as the creation of a Customs Union was in the 1960s.

If Europe is to become a more homogeneous market place, it is important that European companies are ready to exploit the opportunities it will create. That will require managements to concentrate their efforts on matching the performance of the best in the world. Europe cannot expect, for example, to defeat Japanese competition in European markets, let alone third markets, if Japanese research, development and investment budgets continue to dwarf those of their European competitors. The cash flows from past investments of some of the Japanese giants are now on such a scale that no European company is likely to be able to match them. In those circumstances some public support will be necessary, but it is essential that it is directed only at those companies which have a good chance not merely of holding their own in a local market place, but of meeting Japanese competition head-on on a worldwide basis. Our objective must be to use our larger domestic market place to create the cash flows that will allow us to out-research and out-invest our competitors.

Most people would rightly recoil in horror at the thought of competition policy, monetary policy and industrial policy all passing on the scale that is necessary to the present community institutions in Brussels. These institutions have shown themselves to be incapable of allocating resources according to any defensible system of priorities, or indeed of imposing any recognizable system of budgetary discipline at all. If the governments of Europe are, therefore, to reinvigorate the community they must undertake a root and branch reform of community institutions.

Of the present institutions, two characteristics stand out. There is inadequate central budgetary control, and the spending decisions are the result of political deals between member states. Since, for the foreseeable future, Europe will remain a region of nation states, each jealous of its independence, the only credible model for European institutions is one which involves national governments more closely in the decisions of the community. It is therefore a matter of priority for European governments to provide the political commitment and direction through the Council of Ministers which no other community institution is able to provide, and to agree among themselves a process which can address and resolve difficult issues more efficiently than in the past.

The founding fathers of the European Community insisted that the building of European co-operation must start with economics. They avoided the grandiose words which bedevil political co-operation between nations, and concentrated on the mundane task of building a Customs Union. In recent years we have talked of broadening European co-operation to include foreign policy, education, social affairs and a host of other issues. The result has been a tendency for the Community to lose its focus, and for progress to slow down. Yet, in reality, it is still in the field of economic co-operation that the greatest opportunities lie, and European governments would be well advised to refocus their efforts on economic issues to ensure that those opportunities are taken.

To argue for a renewed focus in Europe on economic co-operation is not at all the same thing, however, as arguing for a defensive or introspective approach. While many of the most acute threats to the European economy come from outside the continent, it is also true that many of the world's greatest economic opportunities lie there too. One of the great unanswered questions of the 1980s has been how to unlock the growth potential of the emerging economies of Southern Asia and South America. The next generation of European leaders must answer that question, for although the realization of the full potential of these economies will undoubtedly unleash a new competitive whirlwind into the world economy, the result will be a dramatic stimulus to the world's growth rate, and unrivalled opportunities for flexible and competitive companies from all over the world.

The examples, first of Japan and later of Korea, demonstrate clearly both the threat and the opportunity presented to the developed world by the emerging countries. In the early stages of development, the emerging country needs to import capital goods. At that stage it needs western capital to finance the imports it is buying from western companies. As the development process takes hold, it needs access to western markets so that it can develop export markets, first so that it can sustain its capital goods import programme and later so that it can service and repay the debts it incurred at the start.

It is only at this relatively late stage in the development process that exports run well ahead of imports, and the problems now posed for western companies by Japanese industry start to manifest themselves. Until this stage, although some traditional sectors of industry may suffer from competition from emerging country exports, the trade balance as a whole represents not a threat to developed country industry, but a major opportunity for capital goods exporters.

Furthermore, quite apart from the opportunities for western companies, the development process is by far the most effective way to deal with the ghastly problems of third world poverty. Many well-intentioned people believe that the only way to deal with the wealth imbalance between rich and poor countries is by official aid. Aid undoubtedly does have an important part to play in providing the physical and social infrastructures that are necessary to allow economic development to take place. Basic levels of literacy and numeracy are for example important, and industrialization cannot take place without adequate communications. By far the greatest opportunities for development in Third World countries, however, in both the industrial and agricultural sectors, lie in stimulating market-oriented activity, and in ensuring there is sufficient capital to allow market opportunities to be exploited.

For European leaders to attach a high priority to liberalizing and encouraging capital flows to the emerging economies, and to liberalizing trading relationships with them, is therefore a policy justified both by European economic interests and by the proper concerns of the European electorate about poverty in the Third World.

It is remarkable that a process whose results are so wholly benign should be so systematically retarded by the present international financial system. The United States government has, for example, contributed significantly to its own trade deficit by limiting capital flows to South America, thereby choking off demand for American exports in that region. Indeed the policy has been so successful that the world's richest economy is now financing its trade deficit in part by borrowing from the world's poorest economies.

By impeding the flow of capital to investment-starved countries, and restricting trade in agricultural products and basic manufactures, the West, including Europe, is suppressing world economic growth, and also – by impeding the ability of emerging countries to honour existing debts – inhibiting western banks' ability to finance future growth either at home or abroad.

Nor is the argument purely about economics. Even though the basis of European co-operation is likely to remain principally economic for the forseeable future, we should not be blind to the political and strategic implications of our actions. Similar economic arguments were used by President Truman in the late 1940s to justify the provision of capital to finance the rebuilding of war-torn Europe. Truman also, however, had a second objective.

In the late 1940s Russian expansionism in Eastern Europe was plain for all to see. American plans to promote the reconstruction of Europe were motivated as much by a desire to ensure that Europeans felt that they had a society that was worth defending, as it was by an altruistic concern for European welfare, or by a narrow concern about American economic interests.

Although the analogy is overworked, the success of Truman's policy undoubtedly has lessons for us today. Just as the Soviet Union was expansionist in Eastern Europe in the 1940s, so it has recently demonstrated in Vietnam, in Southern Africa, in Afghanistan and in Central America, that it is today expansionist on a worldwide scale. The Western response therefore also needs to be worldwide, and the West undoubtedly has a strategic as well as an economic interest in promoting economic development in the developing countries, to underwrite the stability of their societies and to demonstrate the West's practical commitment to economic development.

If we can use the network of contacts that survives into the post-colonial world to encourage the emerging countries to participate fully in the Western system, we shall have created a vast market opportunity, which we must then ensure that European industry is in a fit state to satisfy. Although our position would no longer be pre-eminent, we would then be able to look our children in the eye. If we fail, however, either the world will be a poorer and therefore a more dangerous place, or alternatively the growth will happen, and the beneficiaries will be outside Europe. History will be repeating itself and the second Dark Age will have begun.

In his forward-looking approach to the commercial revival of Britain and the European Community, Peter Walker has always placed eradication of unnecessary unemployment as a high priority.

In a speech to the meeting held at the Conservative Party Conference in 1986 he addressed more than one hundred Conservative MPs who had created an organization to examine policies that would effectively tackle the unemployment created by the depression. Peter Walker's was perhaps the only speech of any politician that had as its ambition a return to full employment. He said:

Whenever in this century there has been a substantial rise in unemployment due to a world recession and world financial mis-management, there has soon developed a pessimism as to whether unemployment would continue as a lasting feature of the economic and social scene. For two centuries improvements in technology and the replacement of manpower with machines has created the fear that unemployment would be ever-increasing as technology developed.

The deep depression of the 1930s did not result in lasting unemployment. The economic activity of rearmament, and thereafter the economic activity of rebuilding a devastated world, saw to it that for several decades full employment was a feature of our scene.

We have now had twelve years when under Labour governments and Conservative governments there has been a return to a substantial level of unemployment. But certainly the task of any political party that wishes to govern our country must be to see that that trend is reversed and the horrors of unemployment are eradicated. The debilitating impacts upon the individual and the family of unemployment are unacceptable. The divisive nature of a nation divided between areas of high employment and areas of full employment is unacceptable for those seeking a united nation. The economic absurdity of spending billions of pounds for millions of people to produce nothing retards the objective of providing improving living standards and the eradication of poverty in all of its forms.

The Conservative Party never has and never should tolerate unemployment. It is right that this Government will have spent (in 1986) £3 billion on measures to support retraining, to generate employment and to generate enterprise. It is right that this Government should in the community programmes provide temporary jobs for over 300 000 long-term unemployed. It is right that the Government should have extended the re-start programme to remotivate the long-term unemployed and help them on the route back to work.

I warmly welcome David Young's 'Action for Jobs' bringing to the attention of those who are suffering the ways in which the Government can be of help. I certainly share his desire to have even greater impact. There is no doubt that we must in the coming months make the nation aware of our determination to see that the next period of Conservative Government is a period in which we walk the road back to the prosperity and the contentment that an economy with full employment enjoys.

It will not be enough for us to proclaim the billions of pounds we are already devoting to this task. It will be important for us to spell out the visions we have for the years that lie ahead. Labour's concepts are not, as they claim, a policy to reduce unemployment over their first few years. Their policy in my view would massively increase unemployment in every one of those years.

Their hostility to outward investment would mean that every company with an international presence in this country would base their headquarters overseas. Their policies would also guarantee that firms throughout the United States, the Pacific Basin countries and indeed throughout the world that wanted to have a manufacturing and production presence within the European Community would base all of their activities out of anti-free enterprise Socialist Britain.

Their energy policies will not only massively increase our energy costs, but would in themselves put 150 000 more people in the dole queue. Their policy to eradicate the new participation that the people have in our great industries and return these industries to the deadband of nationalization would have the totally adverse effect upon our economic vitality.

What can we do to return to full employment? Firstly, there is our skill at developing and applying what can be described as 'The Multiplier Effect'; the manner in which the Government can take action to accelerate the flow of investment from the private sector.

When I was faced with the knowledge that for the coal industry to succeed in the future it had to eradicate its uneconomic pits, I persuaded the Coal Board that it was essential to create an Enterprise Company through which they would help new businesses and enterprises to come to the coal communities which were adversely affected by pit closures.

The 'multiplier effect' which that company initiated was operated by a similar company created by British Steel. The 'multiplier effect' was applied by Michael Heseltine in his dynamic programme to bring new businesses and activity to Liverpool. The 'multiplier effect' is being applied by Nick Edwards where in the redevelopment of derelict areas of the urban environment in South Wales he is encouraging new businesses to move into new properties on a very considerable scale.

We now have enough experience and knowledge of the 'multiplier effect' to apply it nationally in a far more sophisticated way. We know it is not only important to think of money to encourage other money to come in, but we must think of the use of existing buildings where their former use is no longer required. There is a need to have on hand management and financial advice so that the new businesses of today do not by mistakes become the bankrupt businesses of tomorrow. The coal industry has been very successful not just in providing the money for the new jobs but also providing the workshops, the buildings and a range of managerial services. We need to study carefully the 'multiplier effect' on the inner cities. Many of our worst inner city areas are in the hands of the militant left. They will never bring economic revival because they have a passionate opposition to free enterprise itself. The militant left have crippled Liverpool not revived it. It is therefore the Government that has the need to illustrate in our inner cities how the 'multiplier effect' can bring new hope and revival to them. The first part of our strategy therefore is a clear and substantial application of the 'multiplier effect'.

The 'multiplier effect' is surely the type of partnership between government and free enterprise that we need to create in a modern world. We know that all of our competitors have created a partnership between government and industry, be it the French, the Germans, the Japanese or the Americans. If they have a working partnership and we do not, they succeed. We must develop successful partnership techniques and apply them to the full.

We became rich by mass-producing for the world. We have been hit in recent years by parts of the world being far better at mass-producing than we are, particularly Japan and the Pacific Basin countries. The new technologies may now enable us to regain some of the mass-production markets but they are technologies that do not require men. In Britain we have a historic background of industries originally developed from the craft and cottage industries that we should revive on an enormous scale in a way which would exploit not just the local markets but worldwide markets which are available for such goods. The application of high skill and the guarantee of high quality is what is needed to revive a number of major industries. To revive them would mean a great deal of training for those who do not have the skills. It would mean setting up a worldwide marketing mechanism which in the first place both small and medium-sized firms could take advantage of. It would mean the possible imposition of a voluntary quality control where the control's approval was accepted as a hallmark of British quality goods.

We should seek a considerable extension of the use of skilled labour in the production of high quality furniture, fabrics, porcelain, glass and on a smaller scale such areas as bookbinding and cooking. A bakery in East Anglia has created a highly successful export trade to Germany. The weight of the Germans of Hamburg is being adversely affected by the taste of the cakes from King's Lynn. Britain could become the world leader for quality in a range of industries and in every one of them the activity is labour intensive.

We should therefore examine the possibility of a strategy to become the world's provider of quality goods, for certainly the market for quality goods is going to be an expanding market in the decades to come. As the new growth areas of the Pacific Basin the Soviet Union and parts of the United States increase their prosperity, as the world tires of the purely mass-produced, there can be no doubt that the market for the high-quality individually produced is going to be a vast expanding market. It is also a market where others could not speedily follow if we have the success of which we are capable.

We must, in looking at labour-intensive activity, have a

clear programme of what is necessary with regard to the built environment. We have a very old housing stock that needs restoring and repairing. We have a lot of nineteenth-century sewers that need replacing. We have communications to some of our docks and ports and around our cities that need improvement. We have hospitals and schools that need replacing. We recognize that much of this can only be done when accompanied by economic growth but we must also recognize that they are themselves part of economic growth. We must put before the nation the clear concepts of the advance we will make as a result of the rewards of a more vigorous and successful economy.

When we come to the next election the public will be anxious to hear what we hope to achieve in improving the built environment whether it be in our inner cities, whether it be the enhancement of our housing stock and the provision of new homes, or the improvement of the facilities for health and for education. We must make it clear that our desire to obtain a successful economy contains within it a deep desire to improve the built environment.

For seven years we have struggled with the worst world recession this century. For seven years against all of our wishes we have seen the rise of ugly unemployment. Our task is to see that the next seven years see the success of the free enterprise system bringing about the eradication of unemployment, the enhancement of our quality of living, and the real contentment and happiness to the ordinary family in this country.

For three years Peter Walker has occupied the office of Secretary of State for Energy in what is the most energy-orientated country within the European Community. The Sizewell inquiry into nuclear energy and the advent of the Chernobyl disaster have both brought the nuclear controversy to the fore.

During Peter Walker's period as Secretary of State for Energy more than any post-war minister, he has campaigned for improved energy efficiency and has encouraged research into all the alternative forms of energy. In an important speech in June 1986 he conveyed his very fundamental thought on the availability of energy in the coming century.

ENERGY FOR THE NEXT GENERATION: THE IMPENDING CHALLENGE

The availability of energy is the very foundation of the world economy. Britain's success in the Industrial Revolution was due to the skill with which we applied our energy resources to the needs of manufacturing. Since the Second World War the fluctuating price of energy has been the most sensational cause of boom and recession.

Oil appeared to be the source of cheap energy. Then suddenly in 1973 the OPEC countries decided to create a cartel in the provision of oil, and succeeded in bringing about the biggest redistribution of wealth the world has ever known. A redistribution that created for Western Europe the worst economic recession of this century, and plunged many countries deep into paralyzing debt.

This century is the first in the history of mankind when a world crippled by a shortage of energy has become a possibility. If this century has created energy problems with a quadrupling of the world's population and a gigantic increase in industrialization, the problems facing the twentieth century are as nothing compared with the problems of the twenty-first century.

Britain is far better blessed for energy than any other manufacturing country in the world. We are the only manufacturing country in the western world that is a net exporter of energy. Oil, gas, coal, and nuclear power are all available. But for Britain the twenty-first century will create serious energy problems.

As a major exporting country our standards of living could not survive if the economies of our customers are ruined and destroyed owing to the cost and shortage of energy supply.

The European Dimension

Our biggest single customer is the European Community. What are the energy reserves of the European Community, including ourselves? On the basis of proven and probable reserves at the present rates of consumption, the European Community has oil reserves which would last ten years, gas reserves thirty-eight years and coal reserves that could be produced at economic prices for ninety years.

This is at a time when 35% of the European Community's electricity is produced from nuclear energy. If the decision was taken to eradicate nuclear energy from the European Community, the pressure upon the available reserves would be considerably greater. Within a very short period a gigantic energy crisis would hit the European Community, either a crisis of shortage and breakdown, or alternatively a crisis of having to pay astronomic prices to those who could export to the European Community the fossil fuels that were required to keep it going. If the Community banned nuclear power it would have to increase its use of alternative fuels in 1986 by around 3 million barrels of oil daily, a figure greater than the whole of UK oil production.

The European Community is more dependent on fuel imports than the United States, the Soviet Union or China and its import dependency is rising far more rapidly as European fossil fuel stocks deplete more rapidly. Europe has to face a strategic imperative for maintaining major alternatives to fossil fuels. The Japanese have had to recognize a similar imperative in spite of having the economic strength to meet the enormous import bills for their energy; already they have 25% of their electricity supplied by nuclear power and within a decade that will increase to 35%.

The European Community has to recognize the location of the known reserves of energy in the world. 90% of the known reserves of coal are in China, the Soviet Union and the United States. Half of the world's gas reserves are in the Soviet Union, half of the world's oil reserves are in the Middle East. Purely on the assumption of eradicating the European Community's existing nuclear programme and replacing it with fossil fuels OPEC would be in command and the price of oil would soar through the $30-a-barrel mark. But even at the $30-a-barrel level the cost of imports to the European Community would increase by £35 billion a year, simply to replace what would otherwise be provided for by our own nuclear energy.

The World Shortage

On the assumption that energy demand will increase by 2% per annum to meet the demands of an expanding world population and industrialization, the proven and probable reserves of the world's oil will run out sometime between the year 2040 and 2065. The world's gas will run out somewhere between the years 2056 and 2066 and the world's coal will run out somewhere between the years 2066 and 2076.

There is no such problem about the world supply of the cheap form of uranium (there are substantial reserves) for years to come. There are also vast quantities of uranium which could be extracted at higher cost. When the fast-breeder reactor has been fully developed, the amount of new uranium required will be very small. The fast breeder reactor technology would allow the power extracted from uranium to be raised more than 60-fold. The stocks of depleted uranium already held in the United Kingdom could, in fast reactors, represent an energy potential approximately equal to the United Kingdom's entire technically recoverable coal reserves. Coal and oil-fired electricity systems have 60% of their costs represented by the price of the fuel. In nuclear stations the cost of the uranium is only 10% of the total cost.

The twenty-first century is the century in which the known finite energy resources of the world are destined to run out. Much of the world still remains poised for industrialization and much of the world continues with fast expanding populations. The combination of those two factors upon the population base of today makes the twenty-first century the century in which energy supply will be the great challenge.

The Third World

An analysis of the position of the Third World shows the dangers to them. Currently the population of the Third World is growing at about 2% per annum, and industrialization is getting under way. History teaches us that the early stages of economic development are highly energy intensive. A study of the acceleration of the energy demand of the United States at the turn of the century is indicative of this. More recently the enormous acceleration of energy demand in the Pacific Basin countries illustrates that one new era of industrialization alone can transform the world's energy demand. If over the next thirty years India expanded industrially, to the situation that the new developing Pacific Basin countries have already reached, there would be an increase of 11% in the world demand for energy. Or an increase equal to the whole of OPEC's present oil production. If China and Africa moved to similar positions the energy demand purely resulting from their industrialization would be an astronomic factor in world energy demand. Many of these countries have little in the way of conventional fossil fuels, and they must import.

Declining fossil fuel resources combined with increasing world demand will create pressure upon gas, coal and oil prices which would make the energy requirements of the third world quite beyond their means. The real challenge of the next decades is to see whether we can develop energy resources which will enable the third world to develop their economies and so eradicate poverty. It will not be done without cheap energy.

International agencies and energy forecasters have assumed that by about 2030 nuclear power would need to supply at least 15 to 20% of the world's energy needs. If it were decided this would not happen and we needed to replace nuclear power with other forms of power which are available, to provide the required increase in oil supplies we would need to discover new oil reserves of the scale of the North Sea every two years. Or if we decided to turn to coal we would need to discover a new coal field of the scale of the vast Columbian coal fields every six months. Discoveries on this scale could not happen.

The Alternative Forms of Energy

The world seeks alternative forms of energy. The only form available on any scale is that of nuclear energy. The incident at Chernobyl activated the fear of the unknown. It reminded us that a major accident can spread danger over a wide area. A form of energy linked to a form of weapon which is the most destructive in the history of mankind stimulates fear. Understandably we would like to opt for a different alternative, an alternative that had total safety if such a thing existed, and could harness some of the world's natural energy movements. British governments and other governments throughout the world have devoted considerable resources to such a search.

A country like Japan, financially and economically strong but having to import most of its energy has poured millions and millions of financial resources into research and development work on alternative forms of energy.

(i) The sun Solar energy has been explored in the Southern United States, in Japan, and in countries in the Middle East but no major breakthrough has taken place.

(ii) The wind We have carefully researched the potential for harnessing the wind. We are building a windmill, at a cost of £16 million, in one of the most windy parts of the United Kingdom. This will produce electricity, but at a cost far greater than the usual cost of electricity. If we develop this system and bring down the cost to a third or a quarter of the present costs there is still no way that it could meet our own energy demands. The typical windmill designed to harness electricity on any potential scale is a machine which has rotors of 60–100 metres diameter, is built on a tower 100 metres high and has a noise equivalent to a helicopter. It is not the attractive windmill of the more romantic type that we remember from the days gone by. It has to be located in an area where there are not just winds but frequent winds. These of course would be on some of the finest environmental sites of the United Kingdom. They cannot generate electricity when the winds are too low, and they cannot be allowed to

generate electricity when the winds are too high, so there is no guarantee of the timing or of the availability of the supply, and even the most optimistic proponents of doing more to harness the wind agree that after forty years of successful exploitation they might contribute 2% of our electricity supply.

(iii) The tides There is excitement about the potential of harnessing the tides, and the Government has supported exploration of the possibilities of a tidal barrage scheme on the Severn Estuary. We are also continuing to look at wave power more generally.

If the Severn Barrage Scheme was completed it would harness the second greatest opportunity for tidal power in the whole of the world. There are no similar opportunities available in Western Europe and if the Severn scheme was eventually completed – and it could not be completed before the end of the century – the maximum it could produce would be 5% of Britain's current electricity demand, or an amount equivalent to one-fifth of the increase in electricity demand that had taken place before its construction was completed.

Tidal power also has its problems. You only have daily peak loads you do not have the consistency of supply; tidal electricity will not coincide with the peak loads of demands.

We should take advantage of a tidal system if it is found to be at all viable. But even if it was viable in the Severn, and we looked at all the other potentially viable places such as the Mersey in the United Kingdom, the total contribution of using every tidal estuary that could be tolerably used would be, at the maximum, an 8% contribution to our current electricity demand, equivalent to meeting the increased demand of electricity for a four-year period.

(iv) Geothermal energy We have hopes that we can obtain useful energy from the hot dry rocks below the earth's surface and have recently substantially increased our research programme. Our experiments into geothermal energy have gone well, but they are far away from producing anything that can be commercially applied. There is plenty of heat

below the earth's surface, the difficult task is extracting that heat and providing the energy where it is required.

To summarize, if we look at all the most promising sources of renewable energy supplies, solar, hydro, tidal, wind, waves and geothermal, they could in combination contribute a proportion of energy needed to meet our increased electricity demand but it would be but a small proportion of the increased demand and nothing to replace the present demand, more than 20% of which is met by nuclear energy.

Energy Efficiency

Could our problems be solved by improved energy efficiency? There is no stronger advocate of energy efficiency than myself. I have mobilized the biggest campaign for energy efficiency that has ever taken place in post-war Britain. As a result I hope that in the coming years we can reduce our demand to 20% below what it would otherwise be, but we must recognize that demand constantly increases. Over the last thirty-five years we have improved our energy efficiency by 35% but we have increased our demand for all energy by 37%.

If we can improve our energy efficiency by 20% using all of the high technologies available to us and at the cost of some £20–30 billion of investment, we will have made a substantial contribution to meeting the increasing energy needs of the country rather than reducing the net amount that we need to use. We must also consider very carefully the possibilities of combined heat and power and we are studying the economic potential of an area which could well improve the efficient use of energy in a whole range of locations.

The Nuclear Programme

As many countries in the world have turned to nuclear energy as the only viable source of energy for the future, investment of about £10 billion a year on average in nuclear power stations has been taking place. If, by the year 2050 the world's energy requirements have expanded at any normal rate of expansion, and of that world demand only 25% of electricity is generated from nuclear power, there will be a market for nuclear fuel services worth £25 billion a year and capital investment in power stations of £20 billion a year.

One of the areas of major economic growth and activity is therefore likely to be the world's provision of nuclear energy. Britain is well equipped to have an important share of that market place; we have the skilled engineers, we have the nuclear scientists, we have the skills in manufacturing and reprocessing nuclear fuel.

The worldwide programmes involving nuclear power could add substantially to Britain's economic strength. It would certainly be very much to the detriment of British engineering and many British companies if it was the French, the Germans, the Japanese and the Americans who were at the forefront of this market. Not only would it be a loss of the nuclear markets themselves. The loss of that volume of business and that volume of research and development programmes compared with our rivals would mean that British engineering and science would be pushed far behind, with a catastrophic effect on jobs and prosperity in this country.

The world will continue with nuclear energy. A number of countries are already so committed to nuclear energy they could not abandon it: France with 65% of electricity generated by nuclear power; Belgium 63%; West Germany 30% and rising. Countries that are major economic rivals such as the United States and Japan and the Pacific Basin intend to increase their nuclear power by 40% over the coming decade. The Soviet Union plans to double its nuclear capacity over the next five years and has announced confirmation of this programme after the Chernobyl disaster. China is embarking upon a major nuclear programme and recognizes that the economic expansion they are engaged in is totally dependent upon nuclear energy in spite of their own vast resources of coal, oil and gas. The Chinese Government has confirmed since Chernobyl that nuclear energy remains an essential ingredient of China's future economic growth.

Temporary Expedients or Permanent Solutions?
Democracy leads to the temptation to go for the popular temporary expedient rather than the more difficult permanent solution. In the immediate reaction to a disaster like Chernobyl, it is easy for the politician to say we must eradicate this form of danger to human life.

This may well bring immediate short-term political popularity from those who would like to believe that the energy they require to maintain their jobs and their standard of living will be forthcoming from other means that are safe and will be available.

What are the needs of generations yet to come? Those opposed to nuclear energy correctly question the dangers to future generations of continuing with nuclear power as a form of energy. Why should we leave nuclear waste for generations yet to come as we were left the slagheaps of the coal industry? They question the danger from accidents at power stations built today and having their accidents in the future. These are problems that can be and are being met by the ability of man. The volume of nuclear waste, even given the enormous expansion of nuclear energy that is likely to take place in the next century, is of a scale and a size easily containable and managed.

Safety
If in the first quarter of a century of a new form of energy there has been such a remarkable worldwide safety record, it should be within the power of man to see that the highest possible international safety standards are enforced in the years ahead.

Every form of energy has its element of risk to human life. The Industrial Revolution was created upon the growth of the coal industry. But a terrible price was paid for the extraction of the energy that the nation needed. Between 1873 and 1938 80 000 were killed in coal mining accidents. Many more thousands were crippled for life, others suffered the horror of and death from pneumoconiosis and other lung diseases. Tens of thousands were killed during this period by smoke and by smog, and there is no doubt that the prime cause of lung cancer and bronchial diseases in the period prior to the clean air legislation must have been the massive coal burn.

Gas is now one of our safest industries, but in its earlier decades it was anything but safe. Thousands were killed by explosion and gas poisoning.

Nuclear power had to be different, for it was recognized from the beginning that a major nuclear accident could do harm to a substantial number of human beings compared with the individual deaths and accidents of other forms of energy. The nuclear industry in its first phase of application has proved to be more safe for its employees than the safety that is enjoyed in any normal manufacturing process.

The higher standards of safety required have meant that from the earliest days of civil nuclear power there has been a skilled safety Inspectorate. The Health and Safety Executive's Nuclear Installations Inspectorate comprises some of the most talented and scientifically skilled people in the country, who, quite independent of Government and the industry, exercise a tight and tough safety control of all that takes place.

Such is the desire to obtain the highest standards of safety that before making a decision as to whether to build a PWR reactor in Britain, it was decided that there should be the most intensive independent inquiry that has ever taken place in this country. Sir Frank Layfield listened to the views of all those that wished to put a case for or against the project. He has been responsible for the most detailed examination of all of the safety factors ever made, and it is only after such a report that Britain will make a decision as to whether this form of reactor should be used or not.

In Britain for twenty-five years the civil nuclear industry has steadily provided an increasing volume of our electricity. It now provides 20% of our electricity requirement, and with those stations due for commissioning in the near future, a quarter of Britain's electricity will come from nuclear power. The quarter of a century of build-up to providing a quarter of our electricity, has been a quarter of a century with a remarkable safety record with no serious threat of any description to either customer or employee. Such a record could create complacency but there cannot be complacency when in another part of the world, the Soviet Union, an accident takes place on the scale of Chernobyl.

International Standards

The Chernobyl incident has focused attention upon the crucial need for proper international standards in nuclear safety. If the world is destined to have the greatest growth of nuclear energy in the first half of the next century, then we must create the highest standards of international collaboration for nuclear safety. No person would agree to continue with nuclear energy if there was evidence of a strong likelihood that this would prove dangerous to substantial numbers of human beings. Certainly no person with young children or grandchildren would agree to continue with such a danger, but looking at the safety record of the nuclear industry there is no such evidence. It is correct to question the impact of nuclear energy on generations yet to come, but we must also ask ourselves about the impact of the abandonment of nuclear power for generations to come.

The Impending Challenge

On any projection of world energy needs, there is no way of meeting those needs in the coming decades without the emergence of a substantial contribution from nuclear power. If that contribution is not forthcoming, it will be the wealthier and richer countries of the world that will pay the high prices required for what remains of the finite energy resources. As those resources disappear the price will soar to higher levels. It will be the poorer countries of the world that will suffer the most. Nobody can argue a passionate and moral belief for the emergence of higher living standards in the third world and argue that they will take the gamble of creating the most massive energy crisis yet known to man in the early decades of the next century. A number of nations with substantial finite resources of energy will benefit, but any examination of third world needs shows that the majority of the world's population would suffer.

The western world took for granted until 1973 that cheap energy supplies would be available to create manufacturing strength upon which new standards of living would be achieved. The shock of 1973 taught the western world that severe recession and unemployment on a massive scale could be achieved by a major adjustment in the price of one form of energy upon which it was dependent. That recession has been nothing compared with the recessions that could be created if we moved into the coming decades eradicating the nuclear alternative as a form of our energy supplies.

For those who want enhanced standards of living in western Europe, such enhancement would be impossible. For those who purely want to maintain the existing high living standards that we enjoy, the maintenance of those living standards would be impossible. The decision to eradicate nuclear energy is not a minor decision. The availability of world energy supplies makes it clear that only nuclear energy can meet the pressing needs of the coming decades.

We should and will seek other alternatives and additional sources. Research and development work must continue. Britain will press for greater international collaboration in the search for safe and reliable forms of energy to meet the future needs of mankind. There are no alternatives that are likely to be available within the near future. There is a pressing need for improved energy efficiency. We are currently taking the lead in Western Europe and are doing more than any other nation in the world. We will seek a further European campaign and international collaboration in research to diminish the need for energy by improved efficiency. This should and must be done, but the totality of what is available from alternative energy and from improved efficiency does not begin to meet the increased demand for energy and the reduction in finite resources of energy that is going to take place.

We will seek international collaboration in the application

of new skills to operate nuclear power as a source of energy safer than any other form of energy known to man. Britain has the technical, engineering and scientific skills to do this. We must see that there is international collaboration in all safety developments; we must see that there is an international standard for inspection of all nuclear plants. There must be stringent international standards for dealing with incidents no matter how minor. Britain will continue to press for the International Atomic Energy Agency to have the resources to achieve these objectives.

If the skill of the human race secures safe nuclear energy we will have a form of energy that is environmentally better than any other form of energy known to man. Energy that will not pollute the air that we breathe as other fuels have always polluted our air. It will be the most economic form of energy yet known to man. It will be the most transferrable form of energy yet known to man, transferred to countries with large populations in need of energy. The provision of nuclear energy to mankind has its challenges and dangers but they can and will be met. The eradication of nuclear energy has dangers that cannot be met. The Third World could not enhance its living standards. The developed world would plunge to lower living standards. If we care about the standards of living of generations yet to come we must meet the challenges of the nuclear age and not retreat into the irresponsible course of leaving our children and grandchildren a world in deep and probably irreversible decline.

26 June 1986

In December 1986 Peter Walker was responsible for the transfer of ownership of British Gas from the state to the people. Five million ordinary people in Britain took a direct stake in their industry, in which they had no individual influence throughout the forty years of nationalization. Peter Walker saw this as being one part of a whole programme to let the people participate.

He has always approved of the dictum of Lord Randolph Churchill that the Tory Party should 'trust the people'. In

1985 he made what was considered to have been a highly controversial speech when he addressed the Annual Dinner of the Tory Reform Group during the Conservative Party Conference at Blackpool. His simple message was that the Tory Party was all about understanding the aspirations of the decent ordinary families of Britain. He argued:

There are lessons to be learned from Harold Macmillan's landslide victory in 1959. He too was at the bottom of the polls and losing by-elections two years earlier. When he came to the electorate it was with full employment and he was able to say to the ordinary family in Britain that they were genuinely enjoying better living standards. Many ordinary families were getting their first television, their first motor car and improving housing conditions. It was a time when the people witnessed that negotiations in Moscow, negotiated from strength and not from weakness, could have their success.

It was a time when we could illustrate to perfection that the combination of Tory economic growth and Tory determination to keep peace provided our people with a government that met their aspirations.

A Parliamentary democracy has as its fundamental objective the creation of a happy society for all of its citizens, a society in which everyone rejoices in their birthright of being a citizen of his country.

If we are to win we must appear to be the party that comprehends and shares and speaks for the aspirations of decent, patriotic people who form the majority of our fellow countrymen. We need to regenerate our roots among these decent folk, the ordinary citizens, those who typically live in two- or three-bedroomed semi-detached houses, owner-occupied or on council estates. That is the bed-rock support of the modern Tory Party, and we become estranged from it at our peril. After six years in Government we must not give the impression that we have stopped listening to ordinary families because what they have to say is the key to true Tory strategy. We need to consider in every policy that ministers prepare the impact that policy will have upon these families. If we neglect them there is a danger they will become beguiled by Neil Kinnock or the Alliance, even though deep down they know the Tory Party is their natural home.

What are the aspirations of these families? They are Tory aspirations. There is an emphasis on family life; on a decent reward for a good day's work; on an education in state schools which will give their children opportunities they themselves never had; on a caring state which provides for the sick and the old; and on a love of country and a willingness to see it properly defended.

These are feelings and aspirations which have caused ordinary families to vote Tory in their millions in the post-war years. But I sense that many now find the Government, their Government, remote, perhaps uncaring, about what concerns them and too obsessed with matters which do not concern them.

It need not be a massive task. After all, they want what Tories have always wanted. But it needs a re-emphasis, a rekindling of their concerns. They are not moved by the latest definition of the money supply, or the Government's ability to hit it, or not, as the case may be. They are not entranced by movements in the public sector borrowing requirements, especially when its movement, up or down, has so little effect upon them. They have been Tories precisely because the Tory Party has been traditionally non-ideological and anti-theoretical. If they wanted theory and ideology they could get them by the bucketful from Labour.

Their interests are far more practical, and the Government must show renewed interest in them. They will measure our political success or failure by the practical impact our policies have on their daily lives and because of their genuine sense of patriotism the impact that our policies have on the future and the safety of their country.

A decent home, a decent job, good schools for their children, grandparents not in distress: that is what brings happiness to decent families and is what the Tory Party must recommit itself to achieve. But their concerns are not narrow.

They want Britain to walk tall in the world. Their families have memories of the last war. They want no dictator, Fascist or Communist, to be a basic threat to their way of life.

They want to see their country defended and worry that Labour does not. They want to end the arms race but not at the cost of making the world less safe for the democracies. They want to see a reinvigorated Britain playing its role in great events once more.

The international challenges of the 1990s are enormous. The Tory Government with the enthusiastic support of the ordinary people of Britain could achieve an unparalleled decade of economic strength and political influence. The European Community can be transformed from the bickerings of the past to a new international purpose in the future to become the strongest economic and trading force in the history of man with the military strength to force the Soviet Union to the disarmament table.

That is the wider vision of the family living in the three-bedroomed semi-detached house and it accords with our aspirations. It looks to a British and a European renaissance in the decade ahead. We must not let them down.

The next two years are the basis of a major political struggle. To win that struggle the Tory Party must be a party that meets the aspirations of the ordinary people of Britain and with that strength there is nothing we cannot achieve.

A year later at the Bournemouth Conference there was not the same need to repeat this message as minister after minister in areas such as Social Services, Housing and job creations programmes outlined the actions that they were pursuing to meet the aspirations of the ordinary families.

But Peter Walker sees a whole range of opportunities in the coming decade to move the people's participation in the wealth, commerce and amenities of their nation to a greater degree than any previously conceived. He sees it as a theme that will bring to the family the full benefit of economic success and create a more civilized and enlightened society. He spelled out this theme in his lecture 'Trust the People – The Participating Society' at Cambridge University on 3rd March, 1987.

A century ago Lord Randolph Churchill urged the Conservative party "to trust the people". We have always been at our best and most successful when we have been seen to share the aspirations of the people.

The aspirations of our people are good aspirations. They want their country to succeed and to be secure from any would-be aggressor. They want a decent home for their family, a good education for their children, a reliable health service if they are ill, a job to do and better treatment of the elderly, the handicapped and the poor. These aspirations, if fulfilled, create a good and civilised society.

If we are to trust the people we should see that it is the people who have more control over the destines of themselves and their families. To do this we need to move wealth from the politician and the bureaucrat to the people. We need to see that every family has a fair opportunity to create wealth for their family. We need radical policies to see that ownership is spread amongst the people of our country.

I was a disciple of Iain MacLeod's. When he first became Shadow Chancellor of the Exchequer, he made me his deputy.

One of his greatest visions was the creation of a capital-owning society. Iain recognized that if free enterprise was to succeed in a modern democracy, it was vital that everybody has the opportunity to participate in ownership.

Free-enterprise nineteenth-century Britain created a staggering enlargement of Britain's commerce, trade and prosperity.

But in those days the manager and the proprietor were frequently the same person. Tough entrepreneurs, often with considerable engineering skills, exploited the markets, both at home and throughout the Empire. Entrepreneurs who had built most of the railways of the world, many of the power stations of the world and created for themselves and their families vast wealth.

It was not, however, a system that allowed those who were employed to participate. As British capitalism developed, the institutional investor played an increasing role. Many of the wealthy families created in the Industrial Revolution did not pass on the skills needed to run a modern business to their children. The professional manager became more important, and in this century we have seen a steady separation of proprietorship and management.

We need to look afresh at our free enterprise system, so as to reintroduce more direct participation by individuals. The rewards of successful management should be as good as the rewards of successful proprietorship. A new generation of entrepreneurs must be encouraged.

In the last seven years one remarkable revolution has taken place, one achieved by the Government's decision to embark upon a major programme of privatization. As the minister with the widest experience of nationalized industries due to the Cabinet offices I have held, I was anxious to see that we eradicated the disadvantages of nationalization and replace them with the advantages of free enterprise.

Nationalization has never allowed the participation of the people. The employees, the customers and the individual citizen had no sense of participation. Nationalized industries were in the hands of whatever politicians happened to head the department sponsoring a nationalized industry. Politicians devoid of commercial skills or experience. Politicians imposing decisions on capital investment programmes and pricing policies to satisfy the dictat of the Treasury rather than the requirements of the industry.

The objective of privatization has been to transfer power from the politician and the bureaucrat to the people. We have succeeded on a staggering scale. In major industries, ordinary families have become the owners. No longer are the destinies of these industries in the control of the politician, they are under the control of managers with a desire to succeed. In the process we have spread share ownership all over the country.

Direct investment used to be confined to but a small

proportion of our people. In 1979 only two million people had had any experience of owning a share. Before the British Telecom privatization, the two million families that had experienced share ownership could be described as middle-class, and many of them were elderly. 27% of shareholders were aged over 65 and 56% were in income groups that could be described as middle-class. Now 83% are aged under 65 and over 65% are the ordinary wage-earners of Britain. The privatization of British Telecom and the floatation of the Trustee Savings Bank increased the number of families possessing a share to seven million people.

The floatation of British Gas created twice as many shareholders as had been created in the floatation of British Telecom, with five million people becoming shareholders, making British Gas the company with the largest number of shareholders in the world, and increasing the number of families with a shareholding in British industry to more than nine million people.

It is likely that in the coming months more people will become shareholders for the first time. In seven years, we will have increased five-fold the number of families with a stake in British industry. Instead of, on average, one family in twelve possessing a share, we will move to a position where more than two families out of every five will have a direct stake in British industry.

This revolution means that millions of our people now know that the purchase of a share is a simple process and is not an action confined to the rich. People with modest savings know now how to participate.

We must now recognize that there is a big new capital market: that more and more of the British public will now have a new awareness of both the opportunities and the problems of British industry.

We have a new element in British democracy of immense significance to the future of our economic success.

But there remains a disparity between the rewards of proprietorship and the rewards of successful management. Take the example of a firm that is able to recruit a very bright new Chief Executive at £60 000 per annum. The calculation of the proprietors of the business is that the recruitment of such a person would increase the profitability of the company by £120 000 per annum, £60 000 of which would be paid to the Chief Executive's salary and £60 000 of which would go to added profits to the benefit of the proprietor. Look at the disparity between the results of the position of each of the persons involved. The Chief Executive on an income of £60 000 would immediately lose £30 000 of this in tax and insurance contributions, leaving a net income of £30 000 per annum.

This of course would enable him to pay a mortgage on a good and pleasant home, to run a motor car; to have a holiday abroad. But would not become rich in capital.

But the proprietor would pay £20 000 in corporation tax and would be left with profits, after corporation tax, of around £40 000. If his company enjoyed a capital rating which was average for the Stock Exchange as a whole, the capital valuation of that £40 000 would be half a million pounds. The result for the proprietor is that he would be half a million pounds richer, and if he decided to dispose of his capital, it would pay a 30% capital gains tax and would still be left with £350 000 capital appreciation net after tax.

The way to bridge this disparity is to allow proprietors to transfer taxed capital reserves to a manager in return for a service contract. The individual could obtain a capital sum for the application of his skills for a period of years. In the same way as the proprietor becomes wealthy by being able to sell a multiplication of his profits for a capital sum.

The Tory Party could produce an exciting and imaginative policy to create real participation over its next five years of office. Just imagine what could be achieved.

1 The transfer of the majority of council houses to the proprietorship of their tenants, thus giving a third of the population who are now permanent tenants of the state a very real and permanent stake in our country.
2 The change in the taxation system so that capital

payments could be made for a guaranteed application over a period of time of the skill of the individual. Such a taxation incentive would result in a considerable transfer of capital from existing proprietorship to existing employees and management, a transfer for which the proprietor could well be rewarded by the far greater thrust and enthusiasm of those he had rewarded.

3 A further extension of privatization so that major industries that can be run more effectively free of political interference can become owned by the individuals working for that industry and the customers of that industry. A dynamic programme for the next five years would mean that the majority of households could be participants.

4 The educational system should be changed so that all children in their last year at school devoted one week of that year to being told the mechanisms of ownership: how to become home owners, the availability of mortgages and improvement grants, how to improve and enhance older properties in order to see that they swiftly get on to the road to house proprietorship.

The workings of the Stock Exchange, the methods by which you can buy and sell shares, the hazards and the opportunities – all need to be more popularly understood.

They could be taken through all the schemes that are available for the start of your own business. They could be addressed by those who had been successful proprietors in small and large companies. They could have explained to them the role of the institutions and the manner in which a high proportion of the flow of cash funds in Britain are on behalf of the life policy holders and the pensioners and the institutional investors. They could be given at the end of such a week appropriate notes and a guide which thereafter could be up-dated once a year. All in Britain would have some sense and feel of how the system operated and how in their lifetime they could become major participants in the ownership of society.

5 The programme that has got under way in the last five years to encourage the creation of small businesses should be intensified. The Small Business Enterprise Agencies should extend their activities. More frequent conferences and advisory services should be organized on a town-by-town basis and the tax inducements for people to invest their surplus cash into small businesses should continue.

6 All companies employing more than twenty people should provide a copy of those accounts to each employee and have a meeting in which every individual employee would have an opportunity of putting a question to the proprietorship. Further inducements should be given for stock option schemes and schemes under which the employees could obtain shares in the company for which they work.

7 The USM has enabled many companies to obtain a Stock Exchange quotation. There is however a need for risk capital for smaller ventures and the possibility should be examined of having registered a local market organized by a local office of a stockbroking firm or accountants, or a company with appropriate professional standards of disciplines where smaller ventures could register their financial requirements, so that the local financial and business community could establish a local financial market. A combination of these policies would transform the commercial and political environment of Britain. Socialism could never take over industry or housing if the ownership is spread amongst all of the people.

Participation by one generation also means benefits to the next. Another major disparity in Britain is the unevenness of inheritance.

The wealth created by one generation has frequently given enormous advantages of wealth and opportunity to the next.

If we move to a society where a great majority of families own their own home and the great majority of employees acquire a stake either in the business in which they work or the commerce of their nation, then the great majority of families will benefit from a substantial inheritance.

In 1983 more than one-third of those who died left virtually no estate of any consequence. The one-third of our population that live in council houses rarely leave anything of consequence to their children and grandchildren. Figures in 1983 show that 64% of those that died left less than £25 000 as their total estate. If the people participate the position is transformed, considerable new impetus will be given to the quality of life and the opportunities of ordinary families of Britain.

Inheritance will suddenly enable people in their middle age to have the opportunity of a capital sum to give them the means to start a new enterprise, or the opportunity of a bigger investment in an existing enterprise, or give them the chance of a transformation of their standard of living. The participating society of the future would mean a fuller and bigger life for the family. A decade of dynamic progress towards people's participation would do much to create the new Athens. An Athens owned by the Athenians.